THE NATIONAL DIVIDEND

JOHN H. PERRY, JR.

The
National
Dividend

IVAN OBOLENSKY, INC. NEW YORK

DEDICATED

TO

THE AMERICAN VOTER

AND

TAXPAYER

Contents

Foreword

On the day I sat down to write a commentary on John Perry's book, rumors were being printed in the American press that Russia was preparing to establish formal relations with the European Common Market.

Fresh from the exciting experience of reading his views in **The National Dividend,** I received this news of Russian policy-change with a different reaction than would have been the case had I not so recently been exposed to John Perry's thinking.

I was certain that the Russian "move to the

right" would be hailed by American economists, analysts and politicians as evidence of Soviet disenchantment with the Marxist ideology and as manifestation of a dawning awareness of the blessings and riches of the capitalistic free enterprise system.

John Perry would not react in such a way, I thought. Therefore, with the assignment before me, I decided to await editorial comment before proceeding.

Two days later, the **New York Times** fulfilled my forecast. "It's another indication of more realistic thinking these days in Moscow," exulted the **Times.**

Had the **Times** editorialist read **The National Dividend,** he would have known that nothing could be farther from the truth, and that the ready leap to such an absurd conclusion must have fitted exactly the keenest wishes of the Kremlin.

There is no indecision in Moscow about Marxism. Indecision about the ideologies of the opposing economic forces is a luxury of the Western world where we still wage the battle of the industrial revolution, not knowing that the industrial revolution is over and that Capitalism won and Communism lost.

The realists in the Kremlin know about it, however, and realize that a new revolution is underway, the technological revolution. This one they intend to win.

Technocracy and automation are no newer to Moscow than they are to Miami. What is new in the Soviet Union, as it is new in the United States, is cybernation — the use of equipment to make decisions.

That's why the Soviet Union made its bid to "do business" with the Common Market countries. There automation coupled with cybernation has been developed higher than anywhere else in the world. It is access to those techniques that the Soviet wants. It wants it much more than the additional trade that might accrue from the Common Market.

As John Perry brings the world situation into perspective to develop his plan which calls for a vital and drastic change in federal policy through a constitutional amendment, he spells out this very transition from the industrial revolution to the technical revolution.

I had not intended to let this foreword deal with anything topical or of transient interest, for it is my unqualified belief that a century from now the economic philosophy — for that is what it really is — of John Perry will be discussed by thoughtful humans as, long afterward, contemplative and responsible people discuss and ponder upon the philosophies of Adam Smith, Marx, Kissinger and Baruch and Berle.

At this writing I have been a student of economics for nearly 30 years. Much of that time, as a newspaper editor and syndicated columnist, I have been, or tried to be, an objective student of economics. But I have never been an objective reporter or supporter of the unique enterprise system that has evolved from America's distinct, you might even say peculiar, utilization of the capitalistic mode. I have been frankly prejudiced in its favor because I believe it to be the most rewarding, the least-faulty — despite its many faults — of any system ever devised. Perhaps, in recent years, I have been so militantly prejudiced in favor of America's private enterprise system that I have been impatiently caustic in dealing with its critics.

With that background, I say: I wish I had said the things that John Perry says in **The National Dividend.**

To this I add a challenge: Let any person of normal perception read **The National Dividend** and I defy him to be anything but optimistic about the future of either America or the private enterprise system which is America, and the source of our freedom.

Whether or not you are inspired by the remarkable Perry plan for a national dividend for every voter, you will find no where in current literature a more easily-read, easily-understood, graphic, dynamic and dramatic presentation of the values of the wondrous American private enterprise system. To read is to believe, for Mr. Perry has virtually stuffed his narrative with palatable, easily-digested facts.

I can not, should not and would not attempt herein to analyze his plan or his recommendation for a constitutional amendment. Such a happy discovery is for the Perry reader, not the Rogers reader.

Every thoughtful student of American economics has believed for many years that the greatest obstacle to economic growth, the biggest single cause of unemployment, has been the tax law, or the application of the tax law. More onerous than any other form of government control it has sapped the vitality of the most vigorous nation on earth to reduce its annual growth rate to a par with the most backward nations, far behind the growth rate of our allies, and about half that of the Russian rate.

That is why tax reform — tax revision — and not tax reduction, per se, has been sought by so many business leaders and economists for so long. That is why business men and economists embraced and endorsed the now - abandoned Herlong-Baker bill which called for complete tax reform. It is also why politicians of both parties blocked the Herlong-Baker bill in committee and wouldn't allow it to be discussed, for it would have deprived the central government planners of their means of perpetuation.

Needless to say, the Perry plan calls for total tax reformation, and with specific step-by-step instructions.

I am convinced that he is right. I am convinced, moreover, that if the Perry plan is not adopted soon, as the result of public pressure, ultimately it will be incorporated piecemeal into the American fabric as an expedient for survival — that is, if we are to continue our capitalistic ways under the private enterprise system.

John Perry is a successful operator in the communications field of newspapers, television and printing plants, probably the most competitive field of endeavor under the enterprise system. He sells services in a market which is overrun with people selling the same kind of service. Being mindful that it is his customers who decree his success or failure, just as an audience determines who will or who will not be a Broadway star, one must concede that John Perry understands this private enterprise system of ours and knows what he is talking about. If he didn't, the competition would have cut him down.

His book is like a rocket-fired missile. It is slim, accurately-aimed, undivertible, and it delivers a powerful, permanent impact.

—Donald I. Rogers

New York City

Introduction

This book, **The National Dividend,** offers a bold, but simple, plan to make every American voter a profit-sharing partner in the free enterprise system.

In establishing this partnership, the plan also sets up the machinery for coping with, and solving, the many economic and social problems certain to confront the American people in the technological revolution which already is upon us with its computers, automation and cybernetics.

With its foundation firmly established in the production and profits of the free enterprise system, the national dividend plan provides a way for us to regain, strengthen and preserve our individual liberties. It guarantees improvement of the general welfare without sacrificing personal rights, freedom and dignity to the bureaucracy of an all-powerful federal government. And it provides this improvement out of earnings, not by additional taxes that increase the cost of living.

With its ability to preserve these individual rights and, at the same time, maintain and increase the vitality of a national economy which gives our people the world's highest standard of living, the national dividend plan can ultimately sound the death-knell of Communism.

Karl Marx, the father of Communism, held out to the peoples of the world a promise that capitalism was doomed and the workers eventually would take over and own all the wealth, including the means of production. In return for this, the rights and freedoms of the individual would be subordinated to the state. But, as the following chapters show, his theories have proven false.

Under the national dividend plan, the ideological war between the Free World and the Marxist Communist world could be brought to an end. The plan would provide irrefutable evidence that in a free society the worker not only is paid well for his labors, but also shares in up to 50 per cent of the profits. And, in addition to being given a voice in the selection of his public officials through free elections, he also is paid for exercising that right. Even the simplest peasant under Communism could compare the two systems and conclude which is better.

For more than 30 years — since the days of the Depression and the New Deal — our country has been moving toward socialism with the intrusion of the federal government into the business and personal affairs of the American people. This has been done under the guise of protecting and guaranteeing the rights of the people and of providing services to which the people are entitled. All this has led to the creation of the greatest bureaucracy in history and to building up an astronomical public debt far in excess of anything our country — and the world, too, for that matter — has ever known, even on a per capita basis.

Ever since those New Deal days and President Franklin D. Roosevelt's policies of promoting the general welfare with tax monies, there has existed a tremendous conflict between those paying the taxes to provide the benefits and those who have been receiving the benefits. This conflict is becoming extremely critical with the rapid approach of the technological revolution and its attendant job displacements because of the introduction of automation. As a result, fears have been raised that the courts may hold that an individual's right to a job supersedes the right to own property. In other words, that a property owner or employer may be forced to keep a man in an artificial job when there is no need for him.

The national dividend plan can remove these fears and this threat to the basic concept of the rights of private property. It provides for maximum production and maximum profits from investment capital. And it provides, too, that those profits shall be shared equally between the corporate owners and those citizens who make the effort to vote in the national general elections every two years. With private enterprise given the incentive to earn as much profit as possible, it can ease much of the economic agony caused by job displacement accompanying the advent of the technological revolution, through distribution of up to 50 per cent of those profits to the people, i.e. the voters, as the plan provides.

The compelling feature of the national dividend, however, is that it can go even further in modifying and correcting the disruptive impact of the technological revolution. In freeing investment capital from the shackles of excessive taxation and diminishing returns, the national dividend plan would assure investment capital the necessary dividends for the creation of new plants, products and jobs. And, simultaneously, the national dividend itself would be a perpetual feed-back of consumer demand and buying power for a vigorous, constantly expanding national economy. Thus, the national dividend plan with this dual function, can begin taking up the employment slack caused by automation soon after it becomes fully operative, and, at the same time, meet the growing employment demands of a steadily increasing population of the future.

Since the national dividend plan provides that corporate income taxes shall be diverted from their present channel through the monstrous federal bureaucracy, which dilutes their return to the people in the form of services, and, instead, distributes them directly to the voters in cash payments, economy in government becomes of more vital importance than ever before. As this book shows, the needed economies can be achieved quite easily with no impairment of the proper function of the federal government. And, too, the potential impact of the plan on the national economy is spelled out in sufficient detail to make clear how the awesome national debt and its burdensome annual interest payments could be steadily reduced to a level which would restore much of the erosion the American dollar has undergone in the last several years.

The apathy of the American voters has grown to critical proportions in recent years. Much of it can be traced to the debilitating effects of the opiate of the welfare state. Some of it is the result of frustrations growing out of the steady chipping away by those in our government at the individual rights and liberties of the American people. The national dividend plan would eliminate this apathy in its entirety. Since voting in the national general elections is a requirement for sharing in the national dividend created by corporate earnings, it is not likely any eligible citizen would deliberately refuse to cast his or her ballot.

The universal participation in elections by eligible American voters, who as profit-sharing partners would be deeply concerned with the corporate welfare, would cause Congressmen to heed their insistence that the federal government be kept out of businesses competing with private enterprise.

By providing an independent income and economic freedom for the voter, the national dividend would eliminate any real or imagined need for concentrating in the hands of bureaucrats authority to meddle in and control his individual welfare and his business affairs. As a result, there would be no negation of the individual to the state, but negation of the state to the individual, as was the intent and purpose of our founding fathers.

This book proposes as a solution to these major problems of our time, adoption as the next amendment to our Constitution the four sections set forth on the following page. Basically, the amendment would do three things:

(1) Protect corporations by having a maximum corporate income tax limit of 50 per cent.

(2) Protect the owners of corporations by making dividends tax-free.

(3) Protect and strengthen every voting citizen by making him, in effect, a half-owner in all corporations.

Text Of The

Amendment

Section 1. No income tax in excess of 50 per cent of net income shall be levied by Congress on the income of any corporation. Corporation dividends shall not constitute taxable income to the recipient.

Section 2. All funds raised by corporate income tax shall be distributed each year to those persons voting in the last preceding national election in equal amounts on a per capita basis. The sums so distributed shall not constitute taxable income to the recipients.

Section 3. Congress is hereby empowered to put this plan into effect on a graduated basis, but, in any event, it shall be made fully operable within five years of the effective date of this amendment.

Section 4. Congress shall have the power to suspend the operation of this plan in time of war.

Das Kapital

If Karl Marx, the architect of Communism, were suddenly brought back to life and thrust into the world of today, he probably would find himself engulfed by a feeling of frustration and confusion.

On the one hand, he would find one-third of the world governed by a political system whose outstanding characteristic is based upon his theories and writings of more than a century ago.

Yet, on the other hand, he would quickly realize

that while a century has passed since he first developed his theses on the mechanism of capitalist society, little has happened to confirm the validity of his allegations. Although his Communist Manifesto assured the workers of the world that capitalism was doomed and the future belonged to them, Marx today would be confronted with a vigorous new form of capitalism flourishing as it never has before. And in those areas where his theories have been applied to the governing system, he would not see the Utopia he had envisioned for the workers, or proletariat. Instead he would find far greater misery, pauperization and exploitation than under capitalism, although it was oppressions such as these which he had predicted would destroy capitalism.

Many consider Marx's Manifesto as the total blueprint for Communism, but that is not quite true. The Manifesto has been described more accurately as the creed of Communism, while Marx's **Das Kapital** is its Bible.

Marx undertook the writing of **Das Kapital** in an effort to provide the world with more solid proof of his earlier assurances to the workers in his Manifesto that capitalism was doomed and the future was theirs. Published in three volumes, only Volume I appeared before Marx's death. It made its appearance in 1867, nearly 20 years after the Manifesto. Volume II was published in 1885 two years after Marx's death, and Volume III appeared in 1894. Both had been put into final form and prepared for publication by

Friedrich Engels, working from a mass of notes, references and outlines accumulated by Marx.

For a book whose eventual impact upon the course of world history was to be so great, **Das Kapital's** Volume I was generally ignored after publication. Engels is credited with finally bringing it to public attention by writing numerous reviews, some in praise, others in criticism, but all under assumed names. Although aided by this literary pump-priming, which caused it to be read and studied by an important circle of intellectuals, the book never did gain widespread circulation among the workers to whom its central message was directed. Even today, few people can say they have read all three volumes, yet revolutions have been launched in its name and millions have defended and attacked it with fervor.

In **Das Kapital,** Marx's aim was to discover the economic laws of motion of modern society, and to show that these laws assured the eventual triumph of the proletariat. He took the position that production is the overriding fact to which all other facts without exception must be subordinated, if they are to be understood correctly. To him, production, specifically, meant man's production of his means of subsistence — the appropriation of nature by the individual **within and through a certain form of society.** Thus, from his viewpoint, production is always a **social** activity, not an individual one.

For Marx, there were two social classes. One consisted of the workers or proletariat. He contended this class was capable of and did produce more wealth, or "value," than it actually enjoyed. The other class was made up of the bourgeoisie or capitalists and appropriated the residue, or "surplus value," by virtue of its possession of the means of production, such as machinery, natural resources, transport and financial credit. Marx felt this system was doomed, contending the vested interests on which it rested depended for survival on an absolute freedom of competition which the mechanism of capitalist society tended to eliminate.

Marx: The Prophet Flawed

It is here, in his treatment of competition, or rather, the lack of consideration given to the competitive feature of the capitalist system, that Marx struck a mortal blow to the soundness of his own theory. For, as we shall see, **Das Kapital** thus becomes based upon a half-truth, a flimsy foundation which cannot stand before the rebuttal of economic proof and historic fact.

Deriving his views from classical economic doctrine, Marx's system of political economy was built on notions of labor theory of value and the theory of surplus. He argued that human labor was turned into a commodity because the capitalist who owns the means of production also appropriates the product, while the worker who produces it receives a fixed wage. He contended the wage is lower than the value created by the worker because the worker is capable of producing more than he needs for his subsistence while the wage, or market value of labor, is equivalent to the minimum sum, or subsistence wage, necessary to keep the worker in a state enabling him to produce. Thus this "surplus value," the difference between the wage paid and the price obtained in the sale of the value produced by the worker, is the capitalist's profit derived from unpaid labor time.

Marx felt that only one group in society creates value, those who contribute to the actual production of commodities. He claimed that those, including supervisors of labor, who merely carry on the activities needed to keep the capitalist system functioning, do not. It was his opinion that the capitalist's means of production, or "constant capital," such as machinery, raw materials and mineral deposits, had only stored-up value or potential value. Stored-up value was defined as value already produced and potential value the worth that exists before labor is applied to something. A piece of production machinery has stored up value, while the raw material which it will process has potential value.

With these conditions set forth, Marx then followed up with the argument that labor alone, which he described as "variable capital," is entitled to the full value produced. He promised that when the capitalist society was overthrown, the worker would not only retain the full value produced by him, but at the same time would have access to the "constant capital" which all workers then would own in common.

Before such a utopian era for the proletariat could be brought about, Marx foresaw a period in which capitalists' profits would grow constantly. He said the rate of profit would depend upon the proportion of "variable capital" to "constant capital" employed in a given enterprise — the more labor and the less machinery used, the greater rate of profit. However, he also saw competition forcing the capitalist to install more and more machinery and labor-saving devices. In conjunction with this, he contended, the capitalist would offset losses in profits by intensifying the exploitation of labor — by forcing the workers to produce more unpaid-for surplus value. He believed that as competition between capitalists became greater and greater, the misery of the proletariat through exploitation would increase at the same pace. The growing unemployment he predicted from increased mechanization would, in his opinion, make exploitation of the remaining workers even easier for the capitalist.

Marx held that this process is an inevitable aspect of the operation of capitalist society, just as the exploitation urge is an inescapable phenomenon in the presence of competition. He did not feel that this urge is necessarily inherent in human nature but believed it to be dictated by the class structure of a society which compels individuals and groups to act according to their narrow self-interest.

As Marx analyzed it, competition gradually leads to the concentration of accumulated capital in fewer and fewer hands because the largest and most efficient of the competing groups are bound to absorb and eliminate the smaller ones. As a result, the owners of most smaller businesses are reduced to the status of proletarians.

It was Marx's contention that as the number of exploited workers swelled and eventually embraced almost the entire population, and the degree of their poverty increased, so would the intensity of their anger against their oppressors. He believed that the violent intervention by the proletarian class, organized and disciplined by the very mechanism of capitalist production, would, when coupled with the growing contradictions inherent in the capitalist system, bring about the doom of capitalism.

The doom would come, he maintained, with private property being abolished by the expropriation of the few remaining super-businesses by the mass of working people. And thus the dictatorship of the proletariat would replace capitalist society with its super-structure of state, culture and ethics.

Confusion Between Ethics And Economics

The widespread application of the basic characteristic of Marx's theories in various governments of the world today attests to the tremendous power **Das Kapital** had for driving people forward toward the utopian goals he envisioned. However, as noted earlier, there is no escaping the fact that fundamentally **Das Kapital** is based on a half-truth or, rather, several part-truths.

To illustrate, Marx's thesis that the employment of labor by private capitalists necessarily leads to exploitation stems from considerations that have nothing to do with economic theory. That is basically an ethical doctrine, not economic. For instance, the long-standing law of supply and demand quite thoroughly explains Marx's theory of the increasing misery of the workers, assuming, of course, that labor is in greater supply than the demand for it. So we see there is no need whatever to bring into it the theory of value, as he did. And at the same time we note another part-truth, his contention that this is an economic doctrine.

The ethical character of Marx's theory and the doctrine of deliverance of the proletariat unquestionably provided the real power for **Das Kapital** to drive his disciples onward.

Actually, the doctrine of deliverance of the workers is, in itself, a part-truth. The entire set of economic doctrines propounded by Marx in **Das Kapital** constitutes a philosophy which subordinates the problems of human freedom and human dignity to the issues of who should own the means of production and how wealth should be distributed. Irrefutable proof of this is seen in the conditions under which the people exist today in the one-third of the world governed by Communism.

The basic foundation of Marx's whole theory — that the worker is not paid for the surplus value he produces and it rightfully belongs to him — also is a part-truth. No consideration whatever is given to the capitalist's contribution of risk capital and managerial brainpower. Without these, of course, there could be no useful production, no useful worker and no creation of value or surplus value. Yet Marx ignored this contribution.

He also practically ignored the competitive feature of the capitalist system, as noted earlier. Many facets certainly deserve consideration. For instance, one capitalist can employ the worker and be successful, while another can employ the worker, be unsuccessful and lose the capital he has invested. But Marx said nothing of the value employment in the one case and the lack of value employment in the other.

Marx's principal reference to the role of competition was in justifying expropriation by the state of the remaining super-businesses he envisioned after the capitalists had devoured each other to the point where all competition had become extinct. Historically, of course, Marx's theory as to the ultimate result of the competitive death struggle also has generally proven false. In many fields — furniture, textiles, drug wholesaling — there are numerous sharply competing firms and they dwindle in number only when there is no further need for some of them, such as when new products come into the market and new industries grow up to replace those whose output is no longer in demand.

Marx contended that under the capitalist system it was inevitable that the largest and most efficient companies would absorb and eliminate the smaller ones. This, like so much else that he said, was only half right. It has happened in such fields as automobile manufacture, where efficient mass production requires a huge investment and is simply impossible on a small scale. But in many other industries it is often far more efficient for a smaller company to develop a product than it is for a larger one. And there have been countless instances of small growth industries competing quite successfully with the giants in the same field, or mushrooming into large size themselves. (Xerox, Polaroid and Syntex are among the spectacular recent examples that come to mind.)

It is also true that there have been innumerable instances of the giants eventually buying out their smaller competitors, but, again, Marx was wrong about the reasons, at least as far as most instances in this country are concerned. The reason is not a matter of the large crushing the small; it is a matter of excessive taxation. The owner-entrepreneur sells his company in order to take advantage of the capital gain tax rate. As owner-entrepreneur prior to 1964, he could at least in theory, be taxed so highly that he could keep only 4.3 per cent of the top portion of his income* — even less in those states with corporate and personal income taxes — hence his only realistic alternative was to sell and pay a capital gains tax of 25 per cent on the net proceeds. And thus there was one less small company to compete with a larger one.

While Marx argued that the worker created everything of value and, therefore, the worker should own it, the direct opposite is true. (Worker in this context means employe. Such a self-employed worker as a lawyer or sculptor is not affected.) It is the value given to the worker by the capitalist that makes the worker worth anything. It is worth something only if capital has: (1) provided the means of production, (2) employed the worker skillfully enough to keep the cost down to the level where the product can be priced at the meeting point of the supply and demand curve, (3) provided marketing organization to get the product in the hands of the consumer and (4) carried out the entire process without losing money on it.

Other ingredients essential to the creation of

*Until the '64 tax reductions, income over $200,000 was federally taxed at 91 per cent. After the corporation tax of 52 per cent, the owner would receive 48 per cent. If part of this were taxed at 91 per cent, the effective tax on the owner (after taking the corporation tax into account also) would be to leave him with 4.3 per cent of that portion of the original profit, before state corporate and personal income taxes.

value besides the worker include research, study, imagination, risk and executive drive in management. In fact, these are the features that give the worker the surplus value, not the worker alone, yet all were ignored by Marx.

Paradise Lost

In the century that has passed since he first developed them, most of Marx's theses on the mechanism of capitalist society have failed to withstand the test of time. But it must be admitted that they no doubt played a big role in generating the significant evolution which took place after **Das Kapital** was published. He was quite right in predicting that capitalism as he knew it would not survive, but he did not forsee the evolution which followed.

In examining the salient results of the evolution, we see: (1) almost universal replacement of the individual capitalist proprietor — major target of Marx's attacks — by joint stock companies operated by professional, salaried managers, with accumulated capital redistributed as profit among the shareholders or reinvested in improving the business; (2) the workers banded together in unions powerful enough to impose their demands on the capitalists without having to resort to violent revolution; (3) the modern capitalist state which sets itself social goals and intervenes to protect the interests of the workers; (4) a middle class which, instead of being reduced to the status of the proletariat as Marx predicted, has broadened its bases and taken a vested interest in perpetuation of the capitalist system by partaking of the prosperity both as well-paid workers and through acquisition of shares in the joint stock companies; and (5) a general disappearance of class-consciousness and, in its place, a trend toward establishing a common denominator irrespective of their social origin by standardization of living conditions and of ways of life and by creation of equal opportunities for all.

Thus, it must be concluded that Marxism has succeeded in its appeal, but has failed miserably to deliver the proletarian paradise it promised. In reality, since it is based on hatred, it has suceeded in destroying, and not in building.

It has succeeded in some instances where its idealism has created the utmost fervor and its workers have been devoured in slavelike fashion to create capital (in the form of human energy) to build steel mills and intercontinental missiles. An example is Russia's superior rocket power. But since very little Communist effort is made to help the individual Russian, or Cuban, or Chinese, it defeats itself because its whole theology is predicated on the individual sacrificing himself for the state. This, of course, is a complete negation of the individual, and this has created the condition whereby the whole theory of Communism must inevitably collapse of its own deadly negation.

Unless the ultimate end is for the individual

and his freedom, any society will dissolve itself in its own meaningless destruction. And now we have reached the point in history when successful government and a successful people must point their efforts toward the economic freedom of the voters.

The best proven way to obtain the capital with which to achieve this goal is to free the entrepreneur from the shackles of excessive taxation to create as much additional wealth as possible. This will assure an accumulation of capital for all the people and, at the same time, it will preserve the right to private property, which is the cornerstone of human rights in the first place.

The entrepreneur should be guaranteed at least one half of the fruits of his own efforts, if for no other reason than that he can plow it back to create more jobs and more wealth. Equally as important, he is further entitled to a fair return on his own risk. Denied this fair return, his incentive will be dulled and, in time he no longer will make the effort. Then there could be no national dividend, such as will be proposed and explained in later chapters, for others to share in.

Technological

Revolution

Karl Marx envisioned by today a paradise on earth, brought about by a violent, sweeping social revolution which would destroy capitalism and give everything of value to the workers who, by this time, would constitute all but a tiny segment of the total world population.

When compared to Marx's time, life today in much of the world could be considered almost a paradise on earth — not only for the workers, but also for the middle class and for the capitalists, two groups he had predicted would be swept away by his social revolution.

But, as has been shown, Marx was wrong. This tremendous progress toward a more abundant life for all mankind has been the fruit of a flourishing capitalist society firmly rooted in and nourished by the principles of free enterprise, the right to private property, human dignity and individual freedom.

Many of the world's peoples have not shared fully in the bountiful fruit of the time-tested and proven capitalist system. To some in the undeveloped areas, such as the newly emerging nations of Africa, the fruit is little more than a vision, but it is a vision based upon hope that the full force of capitalism will be directed toward the development of their talents and resources. To others in the underdeveloped areas of Latin America, Asia and Africa, where the fruit has been tasted, there is a driving desire for more and there is promise that more will come because the capitalist system already is at work on their development. In fact, in many countries the desire is so great that it provides opportunities for Marxist demagogues who promise immediate fulfillment, which is impossible until capital can be accumulated. In those areas where the faulty, unfounded theories of Marx have been substituted and the capitalist system rejected, there is little of this fruit because the basic principles — free enterprise, the right to private property, human dignity and individual freedom — also have been rejected and there are no roots from which the fruit can be nourished and grow.

Nowhere on earth has the harvest of benefits of the capitalist system been of such continuing vintage quality as in our own country. Our way of life, our living conditions, our "paradise," stand out on the world scene like an oasis in a vast desert. But the promise of the future is so breathtakingly tremendous that the lush green of today's oasis pales into the seared, scrawny mesquite of the desert in comparison.

We are on the verge of the greatest technological revolution the world has ever known. It is a revolution of science and automation, of transistors and computers, of lasers and masers and tunnel diodes. It is a revolution which has been spawned by the capitalist system; a revolution whose force can be channeled toward the production of inestimable value for the benefit of all mankind, so long as it remains the child of its creators and they are permitted to shape its course and development.

All revolutions create problems, and this one is no exception. Although it still is in its infancy, some of its attendant problems already have become apparent. More will come. But none has arisen yet, nor is one anticipated, which cannot be met head-on and solved by the capitalist system, just as capitalism has done in the past when permitted to operate without bungling interference.

The knowledge that these problems are coming and that they must be solved quickly if sound economic health is to be maintained, makes it imperative that the American people — particularly the American voter — re-examine the fundamentals of our capitalist system. They must reaffirm their faith in these fundamentals. They must renew their determination to regain some of the features which have been chipped away. And they must resolve to fight with zeal any future debilitating tampering with these fundamentals by political figures who are inexperienced and unqualified in the field of private enterprise.

The Middleman: An Expensive Superfluity

Excessive taxation is the kind of debilitating tampering which must be opposed with vigor and determination. Its ill effects upon the economic health of the capitalist system are myriad. Most important, of course, is that by confiscating a major share of the profits through taxation, the government drains away capital which could be put back to work in building and operating new plants, which would provide new employment, which, in turn, would create new purchasing power for consumption of both new and existing products.

The politician contends that this high rate of taxation is necessary to provide the people — the voters — with services they are demanding. But to do this, the politician and the government create an ever-growing bureaucracy whose operational expense s.,)hons off a good percentage of the tax funds. The net result is that the people

— the voters — get a fraction of the services, the politician gets a new lever to perpetuate himself and his political party in office, and the vigor of the economy is seriously impaired.

There is no logical reason why the politician and the government should occupy the role of middle-man, or broker, and exact an exorbitant fee for services in this transaction. Why not let the capitalist system, of which the voter is an integral part in both ownership and function, provide the means so the voter can obtain his own services in a way which will create still more means for him to provide himself with still more services and, at the same time, constantly increase the vigor of the economy? That is precisely what the national dividend for every voter will do. An explanation of its theory and mechanics will be dealt with in later chapters.

Meanwhile, it is essential that the tremendous potential of the rapidly approaching technological revolution for the ultimate benefit of all mankind be thoroughly understood by the American voter.

It would be a gross mistake for the voter to conclude that this is purely an American revolution and that its impacts and benefits will be limited to our country alone. It is international in scope. Every corner of the globe will feel its ultimate impact to some degree. With this awareness, the urgency for preserving and strengthening our capitalist, or free enterprise, system becomes unmistakably clear. It must be the dominant force in charting the revolution's course at home and abroad if the full benefits are going to accrue to the people and not to the state.

Soviets In Motion

We are not alone in recognizing that this era of astounding technological advance is upon us. Russia, the bastion of the Marxists, already has set its revolution in motion. The Soviet Union is relying heavily upon it to achieve the extremely ambitious goals it has set under the current 20-Year Plan, which extends to 1980. In Great Britain, the Labor Party, disciples of Socialism in a somewhat milder form, proposed a bold and radical program based upon scientific and technological potentials in its effort to wrest control of the government from the Conservatives, advocates of private enterprise and the capitalist system.

Both the Russian and British Labor programs call for sharply expanded world trade in the new and improved products which will be made possible through the scientific and technological revolution. The capitalist system must meet and overcome the challenge for world markets.

Let's examine Russia's 20-Year Plan. Briefly, it proposes to turn out all the products of modern industry, move the products and the Marxist system around the world as a package, and then remake the world in the program's image.

It is a program with sweep and imagination, and healthy respect must be given to the effort that will be made by the Marxists to carry it to a successful conclusion. A pertinent reminder in that regard is that many skeptics laughed at Stalin's "wild boast" back in 1946 that the Soviet Union would produce 60 million tons of steel by 1960. He missed — Russia produced 65 million tons.

In its embracement of industry and technology, of computers and cybernetics, the program sounds like one drafted in the capitalist system. Its bywords are "productivity" and "profitability," "rational economics" and "investment." And it leaves no doubt that the Soviet planners know just what they are going to borrow from Western industrial knowledge and what they are going to change.

It must be admitted that Russia's scientific achievements in recent years have been rather considerable. And they have been turned to good propaganda advantage by the Marxists. The 20-Year Plan makes clear that there will be no lessening of this campaign during the next two decades. Here is what the Plan says in that respect:

"The achievements of Soviet science clearly show the superiority of the Socialist (Communist) system and testify to the unlimited possibilites of scientific progress and to the growing role of science under Socialism. It is only logical that the country of victorious Socialism should have ushered in the era of the utilization of atomic energy for peaceful purposes, and that it should have blazed a trail into outer space."

The facts do not support the claim that Russia "ushered in the era of the utilization of atomic energy for peaceful purposes." In truth, it was the capitalist system and our country, in particular, which ushered in the atomic age. Through Dr. Karl Fuchs, the traitorous British scientist, the Russians stole many of the hard-earned secrets of atomic energy developed by capitalism. And instead of the Russians leading the way, as they claim, capitalism has found it frustratingly difficult to get any kind of real cooperation from them in developing and expanding the peaceful uses of atomic energy. But the Soviets never have been inclined to stick too closely to the facts in their propaganda. When they take recognized achievements, and embellish them with unsupported claims, such as that about the peaceful use of atomic energy, it is almost impossible for the unsuspecting peoples of the world to separate truth from fiction. As a result, the unsuspecting millions have no way of challenging the Russians' enthusiastic declarations that it was the Communist system which made these accomplishments possible. Thus the Marxists gloss over and hide the real truth that everything they have achieved has been at the expense of enslavement of their own citizens.

The most effective weapon to combat and disprove the claim of the Marxists is a capitalist system strong enough to out-produce their state-controlled system many times over. It also must out-market the state-controlled system many times over, bringing more and better goods within the reach of the peoples of the world at prices they can afford. And, above all, the capitalist system must let the world know over and over that it and its output are the products of free men, free thought and free enterprise; that they have not been cast from a mold by government planners and forced to function without regard to human dignity and freedom. The national dividend for every voter will make possible this strengthening of the capitalist system and give it so much more added appeal that, in time, no other system will be able to exist in the face of it.

The Ambitious Commissars

To say that the production goals Russia has set under its 20-Year Plan are ambitious would be an understatement. Here's the way the targets for economic growth are spelled out:

"The C.P.S.U. (Communist Party of the Soviet Union) plans the following increases in total industrial output within the current 10 years, by approximately 150 per cent, exceeding the level of U. S. industrial output; within 20 years, by not less than 500 per cent, leaving the present overall volume of U.S. industrial output far behind.

"To achieve this, it is necessary to raise productivity of labor in industry by more than

100 per cent within 10 years, and by 300-500 per cent within 20 years. In 20 years' time, labor productivity in Soviet industry will exceed the present level of labor productivity in the U.S.A. by roughly 100 per cent, and considerably more in terms of per-hour output, due to the reduction of the working day in the U.S.S.R.''

The 150 per cent increase in industrial output projected by the Russians during the 1960's means an annual growth rate of $9\frac{1}{2}$ per cent compounded. This is more than twice the goal the late President Kennedy set for U.S. growth. Equally as tremendous is Russia's goal for increased labor productivity. It amounts to improvement at the rate of $7\frac{1}{2}$ per cent over a 20-year period.

There is considerable question whether the Soviets actually can reach their targets. If they succeed in getting much beyond even present American levels in the next 20 years, they will have achieved a staggering result. But the fact remains that they have set these goals and they are planning to exploit to the limit the technological revolution in an effort to reach them. It would be folly for the capitalist system and the American voters to stand idly by and not gear their efforts on a correspondingly ambitious, yet even sounder, level.

Here is what the Russian 20-Year Plan says of automation:

"In the 20 years, comprehensive automation will be effected on a mass scale, with increasing emphasis on fully automated shops and factories, making for high technical and economic efficiency. Introduction of the very latest systems of automated control will be speeded up. Cybernetics, electronic computer and control systems will be widely applied in production processes in industry, building and transport, in scientific research, planning, designing, accounting, statistics and management."

New planning techniques are being widely introduced in the Russian technological revolution. Soviet economists are known to have worked up some of the most comprehensive "input-output" tables yet developed. These will enable them to measure relationships within the economy and to examine and study in detail all facets of various industrial and financial plans before committing scarce funds.

Full Employment—Everywhere The Key

The biggest single problem facing the capitalist system in the early stages of the technological revolution is maintaining full employment during the transitional period between present production methods and the automated systems which are possible through utilization of cybernetics and electronic computers. The highest possible level of employment and its attendant buying power must be preserved in order to achieve the delicate balance between supply and demand, production and consumption, that the newly emerging society will demand. It is as essential to the smooth functioning of our economy as the law of gravity is to operation of a piece of machinery. But this is something government planners can never do without making slaves of the citizens. Government planners have a history of proposing unworkable solutions to such problems. Then, finding them unworkable, they compound their errors by offering even m o r e drastic programs which are equally impractical and unfeasible. However, if the full employment problem is left in the hands of the capitalist system, guided by private enterprise and bolstered by the national dividend for every voter, it can be solved and the delicate balance between supply and demand will be assured.

The two major British political parties campaigning in 1964 faced up to the employment problem in the new age there. Labor proposed to do it with strict state- control and guidance. The Conservatives contended they had been quite aware of the advent of the new era for some time and already had begun laying the foundation for it, relying principally upon the ability of Britain's capitalist system to arrive at a solution.

In Russia, the problem of employment does not take on such major proportions for two reasons. First, since the rights of the individual are negated to the advancement of the state, the workers can be shifted from industry to industry, city to city and province to province at the whim of state planners. Second, since the government is the principal buyer of Soviet production, the age-old law of supply and demand does not function as under the free enterprise system. If supply falls below demand, the Soviet people simply do without, and that, of course, is a major factor contributing to their general pauperization today under the Marxist system.

In Great Britain, leaders of the Conservative and Labor parties are in agreement on one point, as the Conservative Chancellor of the Exchequer Reginald Maudling put it: "We are living in the most exciting and the most dangerous times that man has ever known, and it will be to our shame if we fail to harness the new knowledge to solve the old problems." But on the matter of how to harness the new knowledge to solve the old problems, they are poles apart.

Harold Wilson, leader of the Labor Party, pledged a government which would shatter many of the nation's existing social and economic patterns, produce battalions of scientists to revolutionize industry and set up new state industries based on scientific research and developments. He says Britain will have to adapt swiftly to survive and have any influence in today's increasingly technological world, and he takes the position that only the Labor Party, linking science with socialism, can direct that adaptation.

Wilson told a convention of Labor Party delegates:

"The scientific revolution cannot become a

reality unless we are prepared to make far-reaching changes in the economic and social attitudes which permeate our whole system of society."

The biggest prize Wilson foresees for Great Britain under Labor's stewardship would be the new products and whole new industries that science and socialism are to create. The state would also control the cadres of scientists and reserve of knowledge that his government would call forth and take over some industries. He said he was content to let most established industries "wither away" in private hands.

Maudling outlined the position taken by the Conservatives. He said that while Labor had been talking much about the scientific future, the Conservatives were laying the foundations of it. He said that during the years after the Conservatives took over from the post-war, Labor regime in 1951, Great Britain's industrial production had risen by 40 per cent; investment in British industry had more than doubled; nearly 3½ million new houses had been built; over three million new school places had been provided; earnings in industry had doubled and the people's standard of living had risen more than in the whole first 50 years of this century.

Maudling argued that the answer to the scientific future does not lie in providing more state money or in threatening more state control.

"The rapidly changing world of modern science

and technology is the last place for Socialism," he said. "Above all, it calls for a flexibility and a response to new ideas, and new requirements, which can be provided only by a system of free enterprise."

Britain Clears The Air

As a result of the months of pre-election debate by the country's two major political parties on the issue, the British people probably have a better grasp of the technological revolution and its ramifications than any other national group in the world. Although started in the political forums, their education has been supplemented and expanded by the British press with news stories, editorials and analytical columns.

One of the big stumbling blocks tossed in the path of the technological advance in this country, along with excessive taxation, has been strenuous efforts by most organized labor to prevent automation. This has been true in Britain, too, but this kind of opposition will melt away rapidly there in the future. The Labor Party leadership bluntly told union leaders who had been fighting automation: "We have no room for Luddites in the Labor Party." (That reference was to Ned Ludd, a Leicestershire half-wit, whose famed attacks on machines at the turn of the 19th century helped to inspire roving bands of wreckers who blamed mechanized weaving for widespread unemployment.) With the atmosphere thus cleared as to Labor's position on automation, the average Briton is receptive to all the information he can obtain on the subject. And the press is meeting that demand, as these excerpts from a column by William Rees-Mogg in **The Sunday Times** illustrate:

"Automation has so far been considered mainly in terms of what it replaces. The automated factory is thought of as a conventional factory in which control equipment has replaced men . . .

"In fact the character of automation is not that it replaces a human control by a similar machine control, but that it replaces a system based on human control with a system based on machine control. In every case where automation is applied, even in part, it breaks the old mold of organization. Out of each advance in automation there is a bombardment of consequential change in all the related systems. Many of the consequences still are unknowable, but it is vital to grasp the distinction between the adequate concept of replacement and the revolutionary concept of new systems, a radical change in the whole cellular structure of economic society.

"The need for a broader understanding can perhaps be seen by the analogy of the early motor car. That was at first called 'the horseless carriage' — an extremely significant phrase. It suggests that the motor car is important because it is the same as the carriage, which it is not, and because it makes the horse redundant. But the motor car was really important because it was a new system of transport; automation is important because it is a new system of industrial, economic and social organization. It is important not for what it replaces, but for what it is.

". . . The industrial consequence of automation will be to make it relatively easy to offer the great majority of people lives with easy access to all manufactured goods and ample leisure. In the next 20 years, if this process is successfully pursued, the average standard of living in Britain can rise proportionately as much as it did, say, between 1850 and 1950. Affluence tends to destroy class barriers, yet by 1980, poverty will reflect only a failure to distribute available wealth.

"Information and control systems will also revolutionize towns and country planning; they will change both the requirements and the means. The replacement of office work will reduce the demand for large central office buildings and the residential and transport systems dependent upon them. Computer analysis already begins to make possible a far more precise and up-to-date study of traffic flow and requirements. We shall need different types of city for a different balance of purposes, and we shall plan them in a quite different way."

Smoothing The Way

There is a desperate need for the people of this country to have a broad understanding, such as that the British are acquiring, of the technological revolution and what it promises for the future. Too many already have built up fear and suspicion toward computers, automation and cybernation. They view them as electronic job-gobblers, rather than as the means of creating vast numbers of new jobs, through development of new products, improved products and even whole new industries, many of which can not be forseen today. This erroneous thinking must be dispelled. The whole picture must be brought into proper focus with clarity and with depth. If this is done, then the fears and suspicions will be replaced with complete confidence that through the use of automation and cybernation, our capitalist system can carry us into the greatest prosperity and the highest standards of living civilization has ever known.

The leadership of organized labor must revise its thinking. Complete reversal must be made of present and past policies of opposing and obstructing every technological development aimed at improved production processes. Instead of fighting against progress, the labor leadership must fight for it and keep pace with it. Instead of thinking of automation only in terms of what it replaces, they must think of how it can be utilized to the maximum in creating new processes, new industries and new jobs. And instead of being an avowed and open enemy of management, they must become a solid friend and staunch supporter.

All these things are necessary if the transition

from today's production processes into the technological era is to be smooth and the economic
health is to be maintained. They are vital, also,
to providing another need — a demand for
automation. This demand should call for general
technological advance ranging from quite modest
improvements through to fully developed automated systems. A scaling down of taxation limits
can create a demand which will then work its own
way through the economy. This demand would
materialize if the benefits of automation were
to go directly and equally to both the voter and
the entrepreneur. The national dividend for every
voter could play a vital role here because it
not only embraces limited taxation, but provides
for distribution of a portion of the earnings directly
to the voter instead of in diluted services through
the leech-like bureaucracy of the federal government.

Tax Relief Breaks The Logjam

The need for tax relief and reform in the United
States stands out with graphic clarity today. In
mid-1962, the stock market went through its worst
crisis since 1929, and it was obvious the c a u s e
was that the market had out-paced a sluggish
economy. At the root of the sluggishness were
these factors: excessive — almost confiscatory,
in some instances — taxation; what was widely
considered to be President Kennedy's negative attitude toward business in general, as

exemplified in his blunt attack on the steel industry and its proposed p r i c e increases; and fears in the business world that the federal government's policy of planned deficits would lead to even higher taxes and tighter controls to stave off an inevitable financial disaster.

In the months since the stock market crisis, the U.S. economy has made a remarkable recovery. However, its gains are insignificant when compared to those possible with a program of realistic and obvious incentives such as are built into the national dividend for every voter.

The lion's share of the credit for the economic comeback since May, 1962, must be given to tax relief. The Kennedy administration asked for and Congress passed a 7 per cent tax credit for investment in new machinery and liberalized tax write-offs for the depreciation of old machinery. This provided business with an extra $1 billion a year for capital spending and modified to some extent the widespread belief that President Kennedy and his administration were thoroughly anti-business. This combination of factors, together with Mr. Kennedy's later demand for a further substantial tax cut, inspired businessmen to boost their spending on plants and equipment, which had been one of the weakest links in the economy in recent years. Their budgeted outlays for 1963 alone climbed to a record $40 billion as they moved to meet the challenge of the technological era. Significantly, most of that capital spending did not go for expansion, as it always had before, but for modernization to make industry more efficient and competitive. About 70 per cent of the $40 billion was spent for new and better equipment instead of for construction of new buildings.

In today's economy, modernization is more vital to industry than ever before, because competition is fiercer than ever, both at home and abroad. Competition's tropical-like growth stems mostly from the new economy's technological explosion, which is rapidly outmoding the methods, machines and products of only yesterday.

Modernization steps taken during 1962 resulted in U.S. industry trimming the labor cost of producing goods two per cent. This covered items ranging from buttons to bulldozers. However, earnings after taxes did not increase correspondingly. Instead they dropped from 6.7 per cent of invested capital 10 years earlier to 5.7 per cent, a clear indication that the cost of modernizing comes high and the need for tax relief had not been fully met.

The Danger Of Unemployment

The modernization programs with their automation and cybernation have taken their tolls of labor, creating a disturbing overcapacity for the existing economic structure. Modernization to economize means replacing men with machines, which cost less than people over the long haul and produce more. Additionally, machines themselves belong to no union and are free from absenteeism, coffee breaks and other production stoppers involving humans. Unemployment in the United States, much of which must be attributed to automation, ranged around 4,000,000 in late 1963. This is 5.7 per cent of the total labor force. The under-skilled and the under-educated among the currently unemployed are being turned into unemployables, which they will remain until new products and plants are developed and they take training for the resulting new jobs. Although business leaders are struggling to cut costs by reducing payrolls, they realize that high unemployment during a time of prosperity is bound to prevent the U. S. economy from reaching its full potential.

Some of the nation's top economists believe the unemployment situation will get worse before it gets better. A few have gone so far as to predict a jobless rate as high as 15 per cent within 10 years if the federal government takes no steps to counteract unemployment. It is an inevitable fact that within the next couple of years the new economy is going to be confronted with an acid test. The bumper crop of postwar babies — the record-breaking number born in 1946, in particular — is coming of age to enter the labor force. Only about 40 per cent of them will go to college, leaving a huge volume in the 18 and 19 year old group to seek jobs. That is where the employment problem is most critical now, so this means that where 1,200,000 new workers entered the labor force during the last year, the total will swell to 2,500,000 annually in 1964 and 1965. And that leaves the big question of what will become of them, where will they go? The answer lies in how readily Congress and the federal government recognize the emergency which is upon us and move to meet it in the most effective manner — tax relief with sufficient impact to break the stagnation of investment capital and start it flowing fully and freely.

The biggest danger confronting our economic well-being and perpetuation of the free enterprise system is that Congress and the federal government will not move toward tax relief and reform with the decisiveness and dispatch the problem of full employment demands now. The somewhat limited tax relief given by Congress early in 1963 already has proved that this is the quickest, soundest method advanced so far to get such action. The business spurt this generated created 700,000 new jobs. Actually, the jobs did little to cut overall unemployment totals because during the same time they were being created, 674,000 new workers entered the labor force, just about balancing off the two. However, it did prevent the economic sag which certainly would have developed if the 674,000 new workers had hit the labor market and the 700,000 new jobs had not been made available to cushion the impact. The job-generating force of the 1964 tax cut cannot be fully determined until some time after all of its provisions become effective in 1965.

President Kennedy in mid-1963 appointed a commission on automation to search for means of easing the unemployment backwash caused when machines replace men. The commission will outline the effect automation is likely to have during the next 10 years and recommend governmental action. The President said the commission "should undertake the most comprehensive review of this complex and many-sided subject ever ventured," and he gave it until the end of 1964 to complete its study. This move by Mr. Kennedy was commendable in some respects, primarily because it evidenced concern at the highest level of our government with the most important single problem created by rapidly advancing technology. However, the approach taken would indicate the full scope of the problem has not been grasped. A two-year study would be in order if undertaken after initial effective action to cope with the problem as it now exists and prevent it from becoming even greater during the next few years.

Even while the study is underway, the proponents of bigger, more centralized federal government already are advocating that the government assume greater "responsibility" in creating jobs for workers displaced by automation and cybernation. No one would argue against them if they defined government "responsibility" as simply making tax revisions to stimulate investment capital; or enacting the proposed national dividend for every voter to serve the double purpose of stimulating i n v e s t m e n t and assuring a continuous supply of capital funds. But they don't think along these lines. For instance, Sen. Jennings Randolph, West Virginia Democrat, argues flatly that it is the government's responsibility to help create jobs for workers displaced by automation and cybernation. He thinks the government should do this with an expanded area redevelopment program. Rep. John A. Blatnik, Minnesota Democrat, would double the initial $900 million authorized in expenditures under the "Accelerated Public Works" for projects ranging from boardwalks to barbecue pits and from sports stadia to municipal traffic signal systems. Sen. Pat McNamara, Michigan Democrat, would go even further — he would provide $1.5 billion more for similar new projects.

Gunnar Myrdal, the Swedish Socialist economist whose book, **An American Dilemma,** was cited by the U.S. Supreme Court in 1954 as one support of its historic school desegregation decision, has written another, **Challenge to Affluence.** In it he contends we are lagging behind all other major nations, except perhaps India, in economic growth. He says we are failing to live up to the potential of the American dream, citing a rising core of unemployment and an economic growth rate below the population expansion to support his position. Myrdal believes that our federal government "will generally have to increase its responsibilities for a larger part of consumption and investment and, consequently, for employment and production." His proposed cure is far more dangerous than the illness because it would lead eventually to complete state control and to the loss of individual initiative, freedom and dignity.

One point stands out clearly. The problem of maintaining full employment during the transition into the technological age is far too big, too complex and too vital to be solved with such bureaucratic boondoggles as "make work" programs financed by tax dollars and designed to prime the economic pump. Futile and foolish ventures such as the current "Accelerated P u b l i c Works" program, which some would expand, can not possibly fill the demand for permanent, full-time jobs. Major public works projects like huge dams, military installations, bridges and tunnels will not do it. The brain-children of the bureaucrats can be financed only through the use of tax funds. And tax funds represent potential investment capital drained away from private enterprise, never again to be available to foster growth, expansion and the creation of new sources of tax funds. Such programs work at direct odds with the only answer to the problem — heavy capital investment in new products and new plants. That is the only way new, permanent jobs are created. The national dividend for every voter will assure their continuing creation and, at the same time, maintain the high level of buying power necessary to sustain a flourishing economy in the technological era.

Free Man Vs.
Socialized Man

Sir Winston Churchill once said: "Some people regard free enterprise as a tiger to be shot. Others look at it as a cow they can milk. Not enough people see it as a healthy horse pulling a sturdy wagon."

Consider it what you will, tiger, cow or horse, free enterprise is the system that we Americans have chosen as our own. No one has ever claimed that it is perfect. It would not even be interesting if it were. But the fact remains that free enterprise is what has made this country great. From it have come the products and wealth to give us the highest standard of living civilization has ever known. It has developed and produced consumer goods for our comfort and well-being in such quantity and at low enough cost that we accept them as common-place. Yet, to uncounted millions living under a state-controlled economy, these goods are cherished luxuries, far beyond their mortal reach and only to be dreamed of by most people.

The most significant and compelling feature of the free enterprise system is that its success has been achieved without loss of personal liberties by the American people. As it has flourished, the basic principles of individual freedom, the right to private property and human dignity have been maintained and perpetuated. It is these fundamentals that a state-controlled economy demands must be sacrificed as the individual and his efforts are consigned to a great gray sea of anonymity and mediocrity.

With such clear and unmistakable records of success and failure spelled out on the pages of history, it is incomprehensible that we should be confronted by a growing group of determined and dedicated advocates of greater planning, management and control of the economy by the federal government. Rarely do we find among them men with training, experience and records of success in the fiercely competitive fields of industry and big business. Nor do their ranks include successful merchants, men and women who have launched and nursed small businesses to profitability, or those who have provided investment capital for the healthy growth of our economy. Instead, they come principally from the field of politics where the competitive system does not demand and seldom sees solid experience gained from active participation in the processes of free enterprise. They come, too, from institutions of higher learning, where all too often theorists' dreams are accepted as utopian fact without benefit of practical application to the realities of life. This is not to condemn the educational institutions, for along with the dreamers they also provide a constant stream of new talent and brainpower to meet the demands of the free enterprise system.

The Fantastic Mess In Agriculture

Probably the most notable example of the utter failure of government planners and managers who have meddled in the economy is the fantastic mess in which American agriculture is embroiled today. Mistake after mistake has been compounded time and again during the three decades which have passed since the program was conceived and set in motion in the early days of the New Deal. No longer is it a crude, quite cold-blooded attempt to eliminate surpluses from over-production and artificially stimulate farm prices by plowing up cotton acreage, killing little pigs and making huge stocks of potatoes unfit for human consumption. We still have all these, although in a somewhat more "refined" form. But countless new features have been added and the complications have grown so extensively they now spill over the nation's borders and onto the international scene.

Stripped down to the bare facts, the planners and dreamers, in this 30-year nightmare, have succeeded in creating artificially high farm prices, but they also have created a Frankenstein monster of over-production and surpluses. As a result, the American citizen in the role of consumer, pays far more for his food. And, in the role of taxpayer, he has to foot the bill for government purchase and storage of surpluses so the prices can be fixed above what their level would be in a really competitive market. The artificially high prices encourage increased farm production. This brings greater and greater surpluses, which the government has to try to sell, usually by dumping them at considerable loss, in world markets. The dumping, in turn, depresses world market prices, creating a disruptive influence in international relations. And, as if adding insult to injury, the Department of Agriculture, in trying to administer this unbelievable monstrosity, has increased its number of employes from a relatively modest total in the 1930's to a staggering 100,000 today. This added cost burden, of course, also is being borne year after year by the taxpayer.

Vast concentrations of personnel within federal departments, such as in the Department of

Agriculture, are not only expensive, they are a real threat to free enterprise and, in turn, to all freedoms we now enjoy. They are fertile spawning grounds for new ideas and programs for expanding government control and management. In many instances, the dreamers are blindly groping for ways of correcting their miserable mistakes of the past. In others, they are seeking new areas in which they can meddle. Many of these people have lived upon government payrolls most of their adult lives, and they have created few, if any, "new dollars." Like the leech or the tick, which attach to the bodies of humans and animals and drain away their victims' blood for their own nourishment, the bureaucrats fasten to the taxpayers and feed by draining away in tax dollars the personal and corporate earnings achieved through intitiative, enterprise and hard work. It has become clear over the years that they will resort to any means which best serves their purpose. And their principal purpose quite obviously appears to be perpetuation of themselves and their friends in a favored position for continued fattening at the trough kept well-filled by tax dollars. In theory, they have all the answers. In fact, they have all the answers except the right one.

An excellent example of the frantic kind of fight the bureaucratic planners will wage in an effort to correct their past mistakes by extending their tentacles further into the economy was seen in the May, 1963, national referendum on a new, stricter wheat production control plan. The aim of the proposal was to eliminate any further surpluses. This, of course, is not new. It has been the basic aim of the farm program since the 1930's, but success is still so far away it doesn't cast even a faint glow on the horizon. Under the new plan, the farmers were not merely asked, as in the past, to withdraw a certain percentage of their acreage from wheat in order to be eligible for price supports. They were asked to agree that every farmer would be restricted to an exact maximum number of bushels based on his "historic" production. Now, when we consider "historic" production in such cases, it must be noted that in the 1947-'49 period, the national average was 14.5 bushels of wheat per acre. In 1962, the national average was 25.1 bushels, a figure approaching twice the average for 1947-'49. Under the government's plan, the farmer would not be permitted to use his much higher 1962 production figure in determining his maximum bushels. His quota would have been set after considering the overall production history of his given acreage.

The astonishingly sharp increase in the national production average between 1947-'49 and 1962 was brought about largely by the very price support and acreage control programs the government planners designed to cut surpluses. Employing traditional American ingenuity and enterprise, the farmers simply raised their average per acre yield by taking out of production the land which had given them the poorest yields in the past and pouring more fertilizer and work into that on which they continued to grow wheat.

When the stringent new controls were proposed in the referendum, all the propaganda resources of the Department of Agriculture were brought into play, along with virtually every one of its employes in the wheat-growing states, in an effort to win a favorable vote from the farmers. This was no doubt responsible to a large degree for the proposal winning the backing of nearly every major farm organization except the American Farm Bureau Federation. The government's story was this: "Vote for the production controls and be guaranteed a support price of $2 per bushel. Vote against the program and expect no more than $1 to $1.10 per bushel." The Farm Bureau summed up the real issue this way: "Is government supply management going to be the future way of life for the American farmer? Who will manage your farm — you or the federal government?"

To the surprise of the bureaucrats — and of a vast number of apathetic American citizens — the wheat farmers came up with a strong indication that they had had their fill of further government tampering, and rejected the proposal. The dreamers had created a good, profitable thing for them and, quite understandably in view of human nature, they did not want to lose it. The farmers realized that even though the Department of Agriculture said it was a question of choosing between $2 or $1 wheat, this really was not the case. Under the then-existing law — an earlier product of the planners and dreamers — the government was required to support wheat for those staying within their acreage allotments at 50 per cent of parity, or $1.25 per bushel. The farmers knew that even if they rejected the new program, the 50 per cent of parity support would continue. And in their eyes this was by far preferable, particularly if they could continue to increase their yield per acre and the government continued to force all the nation's taxpayers to foot the bills.

Their Ardor Is Undampened

The disgraceful condition of the agricultural program and its socialistic sway over the country's farmers has not dampened even slightly the ardor of the proponents of greater government control and management. In spite of the preponderance of evidence to the contrary, they have convinced themselves of the superior competence of the central government in the realm of economics. But they overlook one obvious fact. Fortunately, few, if any, outside their ranks share that same conviction. The real key to prosperity is confidence. A federally controlled economy breeds uncertainty in business and industry. Investment capital dries up. Prosperity cannot be sustained and expansion cannot occur in such an atmosphere.

The bureaucrats have caused incalculable damage to the free enterprise system and to the national economy during the last 30 years by putting the government into competition with private industry, such as in the field of electric power. In doing this they have invested literally billions of tax dollars in these businesses. Then the businesses have been managed in such a way that it has taken millions of additional tax dollars to keep them in operation, even though they enjoy distinct advantages, such as a tax exempt status, over private enterprise competing in the same field.

The damage caused by these ventures escalates from year to year. In the first place, private enterprise is put in the position of having to finance, through taxes, establishment of a competitor. And, like the citizen who pays higher taxes to sustain the higher price he pays for his food under the farm program, private enterprise, while losing customers to the lower-priced output of the government industry, continues to pay taxes at a near confiscatory rate so those unfair competitive prices can be continued. Furthermore, a valuable source of taxation, particularly on the local level, is closed out forever each time the government purchases a tract of land from private ownership to establish these subsidized businesses and industries.

Look at the vast public power installations the federal government has built and put into operation during the last three decades. Consider the staggering cost in tax dollars drained from the economy. Think how much more beneficial from every standpoint these projects would have been in the past and would continue to be in the future had private enterprise been encouraged and permitted to develop them.

The story is the same with all the costly ventures that the bureaucrats have made into the proper realm of free enterprise, a system which has made this country the world's greatest. If private enterprise had been allowed to keep the tax dollars that the central government has extracted in these instances and then used to establish subsidized industry, those funds could have been devoted to the expansion and development of new facilities to meet the demands of the customers served by the federal plant or business.

Perhaps at the beginning the products could not have been sold as cheaply as by the government, but this would have been offset by numerous compensating factors. The private firm would have continued paying taxes on the land involved. It also would have paid taxes on new physical facilities it constructed. And there would have been still further tax payments on the corporate earnings. Equally important, the need for a steady flow of tax dollars to subsidize operations year after year would have been eliminated. Instead, the private firm would have plowed back a part of its profits into expanded facilities and improved equipment to turn out more products with greater efficiency at less cost.

And eventually, as substantiated by historic fact, the products would have been sold at a far cheaper price than would ever be possible under the inefficiency, waste and bungling so characteristic of operations managed by the bureaucratic dreamers and planners.

Government should never be a competitor with free enterprise. It should be the regulating force. When government controls production of a nation's products and services, it controls jobs. When it controls jobs, it controls freedom. Realizing this, the danger posed by those who preach more government control and management is brought into much sharper focus. These people seem to feel their mission in life is to take government intervention beyond mere control of the nation's economy and fasten it squarely upon the affairs of the individual American citizen. They dismiss the fundamental concept of our free system, that each individual has the right to shape his own destiny. They are convinced that they can do a superior job for him; that they know better than the individual what he wants in life and what he should have.

This is the same sort of thinking that is going on in the minds of the Soviet Union's planners. The 20-Year Plan upon which they have embarked is designed to create a new kind of Russian citizen. He will be a well-fed, well-housed, well-indoctrinated and well-trained person who runs his machine in the new technological era and asks no questions. He will live all his life in a tightly-knit group, go to closely-organized Communist schools, hear only what the government-controlled press, radio and television allow him to hear and think only what the Communist party permits him to think.

The bureaucrats no doubt will howl indignantly when the similarity of their thinking and that of the Soviet planners is pointed out. If this happens, then one can only conclude that these dreamers have not faced reality long enough to fully understand what they are advocating and where it can lead eventually. The Russian Communists draw a .sharp distinction between their brand of Socialism and Communism. They consider Socialism a specific step on the road to true Communism. After nearly half a century under the Marxist ideology, the Soviet Union only now is emerging into this true Communism. During the Socialist stage, there is a dictatorship over everyone who is not a part of the governing machine. Then, as time goes by and the population becomes sufficiently shaped and conditioned psychologically, their theory is that the tight controls of the dictatorship can be eased and true Communism brought into play because the people will have been reduced to what we would call robot-like slaves of the state.

One needs only to look around for disturbing evidence of how far along the road to Socialism our government planners already have taken us. Public power projects, federal housing, farm production and price controls, area redevelopment

basically the result of risk-taking and you cannot graduate beyond this 50 per cent scale without reducing the amount of risk which an investor will take. The 52 per cent maximum rate on corporate earnings and up to 91 per cent on dividends in effect from the Korean War through 1963 and the resulting sluggish condition of our economy over the last several years are definite proof of this. Risk-taking by capital has been the basis for our success and prosperity since the nation was founded. Men have gambled and had a chance to win. But when government taxes beyond this limit, it reduces the use of invested capital and, in the long run, reduces its own revenue. In other words, the government has reached the point of diminishing returns.

The other basic feature of the plan is that it compels Congress to take the 50 per cent corporate income tax it has collected — or, in the case of a small corporation, a percentage up to 50 — and distribute this money equally to every person who votes in national elections. This revenue should be put into a national dividend fund and distributed quarterly. Thus, a voter would get a dividend check every three months, just as today most large corporations pay dividends quarterly. The regular periodic distribution would help take care of seasonal slacks in business and would provide for the welfare of everybody. The fund should be distributed through the present banking system. Then a resident of a state would receive from his state a check that he could cash at his local bank.

It is important that this money be distributed through existing state agencies. There is no need to have a second set of agencies to administer a system that can be handled by state government. Creation of new bureaus and duplication of efforts are two key wasteful practices the plan is designed to eliminate. State and local communities handle their own national elections. The same set of books used to register the voters and to check them as they vote could be used to prepare the data necessary to the distribution of these national dividend quarterly checks. There are many benefits to this system, not only in preventing vote roll padding, but in keeping current population figures and other data which can be used for security and health reasons. There is nothing compulsory about the plan. It is designed to preserve our freedom and, at the same time, establish certain standards necessary to the present day crisis. It must be assumed that failure to register and vote would be reduced to an absolute minimum because it doesn't seem possible anyone, even the wealthiest, would neglect to get his quarterly dividend check which would be sent to him automatically if he had registered and voted. This income would be tax free.

It is elementary that once the dividends started. the voter, instead of listening to how much money the bureaucrats wanted to spend on ill-fated, crackpot, false security schemes, would become interested in how much money the federal government could save — and thus cut his own regular personal income taxes. In time, with this system operating, it is logical to assume that virtually all of the social bureaus functioning in Washington could be phased out and eliminated. There would be no justifiable need for them because the security would be going directly from the corporate earner to the voter. It would not be necessary to waylay and dilute it in some bureaucratic agency. The voter would become intensely interested in the earnings of corporations, and not in cutting down their profits through excessive federal taxation. He or she would be interested in the efficient handling of matters so as to increase profits, and not decrease them.

Insuring Freedom

The plan is a straightforward, reasonable, basically sound proposition to share profits and thus eliminate forever from the babblings of the politically ambitious, the demagogic tirades against profits — profits which are the life blood of the dynamic economic system through which we have achieved incomparable greatness. The plan is necessary to insure a reaffirmation of the personal property right of an individual, to protect him against the overwhelming power of the state to confiscate that property. Excessive taxation can be viewed as nothing but confiscation.

Without the right to personal property, the right to own land, to own stock in corporations and to receive the possible benefits — without these basic property rights, there can be no human rights.

Much has been said about the Four Freedoms. How can anything be done about the freedom from want unless there is a constitutional guarantee that the government will not take the money from an individual which he needs to buy food? How can there be any freedom from fear unless an accused individual can have the money with which to hire a lawyer for his defense? How can there be any freedom of speech unless the press, radio and television remain profitable and their earnings remain free from federal confiscation? And how can religion remain free unless members of the church are allowed to keep a substantial part of their earnings so that they may contribute to the church? That the government allows charitable contributions as an income tax deduction does not alleviate the fact that it is confiscating earnings from both the corporation and its owner.

There is no doubt that the United States under the direction of the free enterprise system has produced more and better goods for more people than any other country on earth. Therefore, we can safely conclude that private enterprise does the best job of running a business, getting the most efficiency out of its capital and the labor of its employes. It is from this point on that the free enterprise system comes in for criticism. It is here that the critic says it is necessary for the government to insist on certain socialistic reforms which he contends will raise the general welfare and security of the individual. But all of the proposals advanced thus far have tried to achieve their end by limiting personal liberty and by confiscating the major portion of the earnings of capitalistic individuals to such an extent they stifle initiative and accomplish less real production instead of more. What will happen to our tax burden when those in the high level bracket are all taxed out of existence? It then will fall entirely on the shoulders of the poor. How nonsensical all this is! We would all be much better off to let the rich do the work for the poor. The best way to do this is to give the rich an even tax break — let them keep one half of the profits and force the government to give the other half directly to the voters. If you put a ceiling on a man's income, you are going to put a ceiling on his efforts. This man then becomes of limited use to himself, and a still further limit is put on his ability to help others. Why, not let him earn all he can and then make him share half of it equally with all the rest of his fellow men?

The real indictment which Karl Marx brought against the capitalistic society was that our system produced so much we would be unable to absorb it and this flaw would enable the socialists to take over. Oddly enough, it was this fatal flaw of over-production which caused the Depression in the early 1930's and thus enabled the socialists to start taking over in this country. But the time has come for the people to start governing themselves again. With the national dividend, the profit money would be channeled back to the voters to absorb our enormous production, thereby eliminating this danger which Marx pointed out.

In order to bring about this return to freedom, it is first necessary to have a sound constructive program appreciated by a great majority of the people and one in which nearly everyone participates — a plan such as the national dividend. The basic theory and purpose of the national dividend is three-fold: (1) to increase incentive so that money owners will risk their capital on constructive, profit-promising ventures, thereby increasing the national income; (2) to distribute half of this money among all of the voters, thereby increasing their individual security; and (3) to enable industry to return to the economic freedom necessary to achieve more profits to distribute to stockholder and voter, and thus increase the real purchasing power of the people in addition to their yearly national dividend. When the people can go back to governing themselves without the inefficiencies and waste of the bureaucratic state, then there will be little or no need for the hundreds of thousands of hidden miscellaneous taxes that create inflation. Only then will we be able to achieve the real wealth necessary to our well-being. We must get it out of our heads that we need these taxes for the support of unnecessary and wasteful bureaus. We do not need government planners and bureaucrats to tell us how much or how little to grow or produce. The law of supply and demand will take care of all that. And with a national dividend providing a flow of profits back into the voting people, their security and purchasing power will be achieved automatically.

Regardless of how you view it, the national dividend for every voter is a plan of, by and for the people of the United States. It is a medium through which every voter will have the opportunity to receive a direct share in the rewards of capitalism and free enterprise — the system which has produced the greatest and wealthiest nation in all the world.

The Checks And Balances

It is quite probable our political economy can be reduced to a science as definite and mathematical as the science of algebra and physics. Until this exactness and balance is achieved however, there will not be universal welfare, permanent peace, real industrial progress and social happiness and security. The technological age with its computers, automation and cybernation will provide us with the tools to help reduce the economy to that scientific precision. But first there must be universal acknowledgement of the basic fundamentals of the relationship between the individual and his government. The Constitution states the principles on which these premises are based. The problem is to carry out the objectives. The common denominator of all the rights which we are attempting to achieve is the right to private property. After universal acknowledgement of this right, then we may move to carry out the objective of human rights for which we hear so much clamoring. Excessive taxation is a federal confiscation of property rights, and before we can proceed any further this confiscation must be restricted by guarantee contained in a constitutional amendment. We may then take steps to provide for the general welfare, and the national dividend is proposed as the method to achieve that welfare.

A complete understanding of the mathematics of the plan is essential to each citizen, that he or she may better appreciate how it is designed to cure our present economic malfunctioning. Each should make certain in his own mind that he or she has a complete understanding of the principles of economics upon which our society and our profit and loss system were founded. The proposal is an attempt to encourage the capitalist to make more profits, but to share those profits with all the voters. Experience has shown that profits have been responsible for a corporation's ability to grow and expand, to make more and better goods available for less money to the purchaser. Profits are not a part of the maker's cost of a product. Profits are arrived at after all costs have been met, an economic fact little realized, but one which any accountant can explain. Profits are the results of risk-taking and prices are set by the law of supply and demand. There are certain exceptions, of course, such as public utilities, where in the absence of competition rates are and should be set by a regulatory commission as a proper function of government. Except in the case of unregulated public utilities, patent monopolies or monopolies operating illegally in restraint of trade, profits never become excessive or exorbitant in a free society, because competition will soon enter the field and swiftly level off the imbalance between supply and demand.

The national dividend plan is advanced in the belief that, if enacted, it will keep in effect the checks and balances contained in our system of government and formulated under the Constitution. It is these checks and balances which, without resort to dictatorship, have successfully enabled us to grow as a republic under democratic processes of law and attain a national income in 1962 of $453 billion.

When the Constitution was conceived and committed to written form, its creators did not envision the enormous productivity which machines and the distribution of goods have made possible. Consequently, in order to bring into adjustment the overgrown powers of federal authority, which stemmed from the people's reaction to the 1929 stock market crash and ensuing Depression, and to restore free enterprise, it is necessary to add an amendment to our Constitution. This will provide both for the continued incentive and protection of the capitalist and will enable the ordinary citizen to share in the benefits of the technological age. It will enable him to gain possession of his rightful heritage and make him realize the responsibility he has as an equal shareholder in the ownership of his country.

Cutting Costs Of Government

Thirty years ago it took a little over $4 billion to cover the cost of running the federal government. The per capita cost was roughly $32.58. Twenty years later, it took about $45 billion to do the same job and per capita cost had risen to $298.60. President Johnson's budget for fiscal 1965 placed the total at $97.9 billion which meant a per capita cost of about $557.48. In other words, the population has increased about 50 per cent during the 30 years, while the cost of government is about 25 times greater. Even taking into account the cost of two wars and the present defense establishment, a substantial part of this increase is due largely to attempts by federal officials to make as many people as possible dependent upon the party in power for their jobs, to offer as many benefits as possible to obtain the most votes, to faulty socialistic theories and programs, to mismanagement and to poor business policies. The bureaucrat makes a poor business man and rarely has any conception of economy.

There is no doubt that the astronomical costs of the federal government could be cut sharply by able business administrators without impairing the functions of good government. In 1955, federal expenditures for non-defense activities totaled $23.9 billion. In 1962, just seven years later, they had shot up to $38.6 billion, an increase of 61 per cent. Careful examination of individual items shows that expenditures have more than doubled in many purely administrative categories. Such waste and mismanagement would not be tolerated by the efficiency of private enterprise. Yet private enterprise and the American people are being bled dry through excessive taxation to pay for it. Defense Secretary Robert McNamara has given clear proof that government costs can be cut, even in such a sensitive and vital area as national security. In July, 1962, he sent a memorandum to President Kennedy which said: "Based on the actions we have taken to date and those we contemplate in the future, I can report to you that within five years we can cut the costs of the Department's logistical operations by at least $3 billion per year. These annual savings will result from the more efficient management of our logistical system and will not be achieved through a reduction in the strength of our combat forces." If Secretary McNamara can do it in Defense, then certainly economies can be effected in less essential agencies.

An average of the corporate tax collections of the years 1960-62, based on the maximum 50 per cent corporate income tax rate provided in the national dividend plan, indicates that $22.2 billion would be available for the approximately 69 million persons who voted in the 1960 presidential election. This would mean that a man and wife would have an additional tax-free income of $644 between them. In the non-presidential election in 1962, when all House and many Senate seats were at stake, only approximately 51 million persons cast votes. Using that figure, the dividend payments would have been $435 per person, $870 for a man and wife. Broken down further, it means the equivalent of $72.50 increase in income per month for a married couple. It would be much more beneficial than a salary increase of that amount because it would be tax free, "take home" income. With the dividend as an incentive, the number of persons voting is certain to increase. This does not mean, however, that with the plan in full operation the amount of individual payments would necessarily be lower because with the economy expanding from new investment capital, profits also would be growing in proportionate overall volume.

Once this system is in effect and the cost of government rolled back sharply, there would be no danger of a decline in the purchasing power such as brought about the Depression. This is true because the income of every man and woman who voted would be rising proportionately with corporation income. The waste of such costly government ventures as farm price support programs, for instance, would be eliminated and parity would be spread everywhere through the national dividend. The best fruits of the capitalistic system would be shared by all who voted without reducing those benefits by a heavy cost of administration.

The adoption of this amendment would transform the nature of American politics to the point where the demagogues would be replaced by the more able business leaders of our country who are experienced in world trade, mass production, low cost and the creation of the nation's real wealth. The resulting dividend will cure most of the ills of the common man, and so long as this dividend comes out of earnings we are not jeopardizing our future, nor are we resorting to the confiscation of one man's property to get the votes of 10 other men. The American voter's interest would manifest itself in intelligent voting. He would insist on having his government operated by proven experts in the various fields.

The Corporation And Its Owners

So that there may be simple understanding at the beginning, let us take the case of a corporation which has been earning $100,000 a year. This corporation, like most in our society, was formed and operated under the profit and loss system. In other words, a group of individuals, or one individual, decides that there is a gap in the economic system in the various services being provided the public. They conclude that this gap, if filled, offers an opportunity to make a profit or return on the money that will be risked in the endeavor to fill or meet this public demand. For example, the group, or individual, decides that in a certain town there is room for another movie theater. They believe there are enough people with enough money in that community to warrant expenditure of one million dollars, so when the proposed theater is completed and operating, attendance will be great enough and the price of admission will be high enough that the revenue will be more than adequate to take care of the expenses. If the entrepreneurs, or capitalists, or money riskers, or theater owners, or whatever you may call them, misjudge their prospective audience or mismanage the property, or some disastrous event beyond their control happens, then possibly several million dollars of their own money has been lost. This is true because, while the original venture may call for only a one million dollar investment, the chances are that until the project breaks even, much more will be required. The government has not suffered the slightest in this.

Now, let us assume the risk, the venture, has paid off and after several years of losing money the demand for this theater has enabled the corporation set up by the owners, to make a profit. It is important to realize that the price of admission to the theater has been set by the corporation to bring in the most money. If the price is too high, the people will stay home and watch television. If the price is too low, the company will not get the maximum revenue. The price of a ticket which will bring in the most revenue is the one which will be best for the theater-goer, the management, the employes, the owners and, eventually the government. Only by aiming at getting the most revenue can the business succeed. Do not confuse this with charging the most money for a seat.

Carrying the supposition further, the company is now making a profit of $100,000 a year. The corporation income tax at rates prior to the 1964 cut would have confiscated $52,000 of the amount, leaving the corporation with $48,000. Now the owner, or owners, are going to want to get back some of their investment, so they declare a dividend. To keep the example clear, we shall say the dividend is the amount the company has been able to keep after the government has taken the corporate tax. But when this money is paid out in dividends, the greedy government reaches in again. This time it takes anywhere from $9,600 to over $40,000 of the $48,000 balance, depending upon the number of owners in the business and their individual tax brackets. Assuming there was only one owner and he was paying the highest rate, 91 per cent, it can be readily seen that on an investment of one million dollars, the unfortunate individual who had risked his money and had now been successful, was able to keep only $4,320 of his profits. (Under the new tax law the situation has improved some, but the corporate rate is 50 per cent and the top individual rate is 77 per cent.) Such a return is so out of proportion to the risk he had taken that individual private enterprise has been seriously hampered in this country.

Returning to the mechanics of how the voter will share in the national dividend, let us suppose that Congress, through the proper constitutional amendment, is prohibited from exceeding the 50 per cent tax and is directed to declare a national dividend out of the corporate income taxes. To take our theater case again but under these conditions, let us again assume that the corporation has made $100,000 for the year. The government now would tax the corporation $50,000. However, when the corporation paid out dividends on the remaining $50,000, there would be no further levy on the individual or individuals receiving them. Thus, the government would get $50,000 and the owners $50,000. In the case of an individual owner in a maximum income bracket, he would get $50,000 instead of the $4,320 he would have received under the old tax law. This would give him a chance to get his money back in 20 years, making it worthwhile for him to again risk his money in further ventures. These, in turn, would create new jobs,

new taxes, new profits and new funds for the national dividend. As for the $50,000 the government has taken in income taxes, it would go into the dividend fund and be paid quarterly, after the close of each fiscal year, to all citizens who took the time and trouble to vote in the last national election.

The Scientific Approach

Perhaps too much emphasis has been placed on the evils of our present economic malfunctions, but the American people must examine all these facts and statistics in an intelligent search to understand how many of the evils may be cured through a scientific approach. Science has done wonders in the fields of drugs, machinery, atomic energy. But we have lacked this scientific approach in our attempt to solve problems of human and economic welfare, stability of our monetary unit, and learning how to get the most out of our workers and private capital. We are all in the same boat, and injury to one group does eventual injury to another — in fact, to all others.

First and foremost the people must realize that the present evils, the result of an overgrown central authority trying to run everything on the grounds of common welfare and public interest, can mostly be cured by letting the people and the states resume running themselves. With this profit-sharing system in effect and creating an automatic shifting of wealth in the democratic fashion, the country's wage and salary earners will no longer find it necessary to support the waste and graft which are not only creating inflation and unnecessary red tape, but which, because of their vast complexities, are ensnaring the liberties of individuals and corporations and daily hampering their efficiency. We must throw off this yoke and get men to run our country who will not have to be in a position where they are forced to think of politics first and the solution of their problems second. Under the national dividend plan, all of the voters would be pressuring for economy and businesslike administration, instead of various groups such as labor, business, farmers and the aged seeking special treatment and privileges.

Most officials now in public office basically are not of any more or less moral fiber than anyone else. It is only that the present concentration of authority has given them the power and they have taken advantage of it. The solution to this problem is the same our forefathers put to use — have a system of checks and balances. If we will limit the power to tax beyond the point of excessiveness and give to the voter a cash bonus to restore his economic freedom — a bonus which comes out of earnings instead of some source which further increases the cost of living — then we will be approaching a scientific solution to the foremost problem in this country. The solution is a political economy which will permit dynamic expansion of industry by private capital in the coming technological era. Such an economy would show the world that it is not Wall Street which is reaping the rewards of our productive might, but each and every voting citizen.

Federal Budget

Much has been written about President Johnson's budget for fiscal 1965, largely because it broke a pattern of the last several years and called for less rather than more federal spending. It was only the second one in nine years to cut spending below the preceding year.

Of all that has been written and said, however, probably the most significant remarks came from the President in his message to Congress as he presented the budget. He told the lawmakers that in formulating the budget he had been guided by two principles:

1. "That spending by the federal government, in and of itself, is neither bad nor good. It can be bad when it involves over-staffing of government agencies, or needless duplication of functions, or poor management, or public services which cost more than they are worth or the intrusion of government into areas where it does not belong. It can be good when it is put to work efficiently in the interests of our national strength, economic progress and human compassion.

2. "That an austere budget need not be and should not be a standstill budget. When budgetary restraint leads the government to turn its back on new needs and new problems, economy becomes but another word for stagnation. But when vigorous pruning of old programs and procedures releases the funds to meet new challenges and opportunities, economy becomes the companion of progress."

These two principles embody, in a nutshell, the whole aim and purpose of the proposed national dividend for every voter. It is designed to eliminate the "bad" spending and distribute those funds directly to the voters. Clear proof that we have had far too much "bad" spending is seen in the $97 billion and $98 billion annual administrative budgets, which now are commonplace, and a national debt for which President Johnson said a $315 billion ceiling was inadequate. The dividend also is designed to leave available to the federal government adequate revenues to work efficiently in the interests of national strength, economic progress and human compassion within the boundaries in which government is supposed to function.

Austerity in federal government expenditures is a key element in the national dividend plan. But, as President Johnson said, this does not mean a standstill budget or a standstill economy. The dividend proposal encourages meeting new needs and problems head-on, but on the level where they should be faced — by individuals, communities and states, not by a monstrous central bureaucracy. And it makes mandatory the vigorous pruning of old programs and procedures to release the funds to meet new challenges and opportunities. It places economy in government in rhythmic step as a close companion of progress toward greater personal freedom and a far more abundant life for the American people.

Although Mr. Johnson's administrative budget called for less spending in fiscal 1965 than in 1964, it was no different in one respect from most of those submitted since 1950, in that it placed expenditures at a considerably higher level than revenues, thus adding substantially to the already fantastic national debt. Only in fiscal 1951, '56, '57 and '60 did income exceed outgo on the federal plane during that 15-year period.

The mere fact that in a period of record-breaking national production and economic prosperity the federal budget should call for deficit financing provides a convincing argument that it, like its recent predecessors, is loaded with the kind of "bad" spending President Johnson referred to in his message to Congress. There has been so much of this under the bureaucratic planners and dreamers over past years that in the present administrative budget, interest on the national debt is the second largest spending item. It is topped only by outlays for national defense. The interest totals $11.1 billion, the equivalent of 11 cents of every budget dollar. On the income side of the budget, five cents of every dollar will have to be provided by new borrowing.

The astronomical sums involved in the federal budget leave the average citizen dazed as he attempts to comprehend them. But that can't compare with the complete bewilderment which grips him when he attempts to wade through a printed copy of the budget. It resembles a metropolitan telephone directory in size and has nearly 1,200 pages of text, tables and charts. It contains the text of appropriation estimates proposed for the consideration of Congress, together with specific reference material on the various appropriations and funds. Anyone may obtain a copy simply by writing the Government Printing Office and paying the $6 charge. Comparatively few citizens are willing to go to the trouble and expense, however, and as a result not many Americans have any real knowledge of where the federal revenue comes from and how it is spent.

Although the figure most commonly used in reference to President Johnson's fiscal 1965 budget is $97.9 billion, that is not the total. It is only the proposed spending segment of the administrative budget. The overall budget called for net revenue of $119.8 billion, net expenditures of $122.7 billion and a net deficit of $2.9 billion. The difference between the $97.9 billion in the administrative budget and the $122.7 billion total is made up of spending from social security, highway and other trust funds, which finance many specific government activities.

In fiscal 1963, administrative budget receipts totaled $86.4 billion and trust fund receipts amounted to $27.7 billion. From this total $4.3 billion in intragovernmental transactions was deducted for a net of $109.7 billion in total receipts from the public. Administrative budget expenditures that same year totaled $92.6 billion and $5.4 billion was deducted for intragovernmental transactions, leaving net total expenditures at $113.8 billion. The deficit for the year was slightly more than $4 billion.

Estimates for fiscal 1964 show administrative budget receipts of $88.4 billion, trust fund receipts of $30.2 billion, less intragovernmental transactions of $4.2 billion, for a total of $114.4 billion. The estimates on the other side of the ledger show $98.4 billion in administrative budget expenditures, $29.3 billion in trust fund expenditures, less intragovernmental transactions of $5 billion, and total payments of $122.7 billion. The deficit was estimated at $8.3 billion.

The estimates for fiscal 1965 place administrative budget receipts at $93 billion, trust fund receipts at $30.9 billion, less intragovernmental transactions at $4.1 billion, for total receipts of $119.8 billion. Administrative budget expenditures

OVERALL BUDGET PICTURE, 1963 - 1965

| | 1963 | | 1964 | | 1965 | |
	TOTAL BUDGET	ADMINISTRATIVE BUDGET	TOTAL BUDGET	ADMINISTRATIVE BUDGET	TOTAL BUDGET	ADMINISTRATIVE BUDGET
RECEIPTS	109.7	86.4	114.4	88.4	119.8	93.0
EXPENDI-TURES	113.8	92.6	122.7	98.4	122.7	97.9
DEFICITS	4.0	6.2	8.3	10.0	2.9	4.9

IN BILLIONS OF DOLLARS

are set at $97.9 billion, trust fund expenditures at $29.4 billion, intragovernmental transactions at $4.6 billion and total expenditures at $122.7 billion, for the previously mentioned deficit of $2.9 billion.

It has only been in the last two fiscal years that any emphasis has been placed on the total budget picture when it was presented to Congress. Prior to that the practice had been to point up only the administrative budget because it includes most of the tax and other receipts of the government which, for the major part, go into a general fund. There are exceptions in some small amounts which go into other funds for special purposes. On the other hand, the trust funds in the budget are created by special taxes or contributions which Congress designates to be held in trust for specified benefit payments or programs. They can be used only to finance the activities for which they have been set aside. Because of this, the administrative budget over the years has become the oldest and most widely known measure of our federal finances. It is the framework through which Congress evaluates a President's requests for funds and gives various government agencies approval to carry out their programs. The eventual spending is the result of three separate activities: Presidential requests, Congressional action and administration of the programs by various agencies. Thus the administrative budget is used for the control, administration and execution of activities financed by the taxes and other receipts in the general fund.

Where It Comes From

The two primary sources of revenue for the federal government are personal and corporate income taxes. The 1965 budget estimates $48.5 billion will be taken from the pockets of the American people in personal income taxes. Corporations are expected to come through with another $25.8 billion in direct income taxes. This figure does not include the personal income taxes which will be paid by individuals receiving dividends from the nation's corporations. However, both estimates take into consideration the income tax rate cuts passed by Congress and signed into law by President Johnson early in calendar 1964.

The third largest source of revenue is employment taxes. The $16.99 billion to be raised from this source will go into trust funds for payments such as social security, unemployment compensation, railroad workers' retirement and others. The tremendous cost of administering these programs does not come from the trust funds. It is included in the administrative budget.

Excise taxes rank fourth in volume of revenue produced for the federal government, scheduled to provide $14.49 billion in 1965. Other sources of federal receipts and the 1965 estimates include the estate and gift tax, $2.74 billion, and deposits by states into the unemployment insurance trust funds (collected in state employment taxes), $2.82 billion. Customs collections provide $1.46 billion, veterans' life insurance premiums, $0.49 billion, and various other budget and trust receipts when lumped together amount to $6.43 billion. All these sources will provide the $119.7 billion total revenue for the overall budget.

An idea of how wild the bureaucratic spending orgy has become is apparent from a review of the last eight budgets. In 1958, the total budget called for receipts of $81.89 billion, $37.35 billion less than projected for 1965. The government wound up in the red that year to the tune of a $1.58 billion deficit. In 1961, the total budget was $97.24 billion, $22.50 billion less than for 1965. And again there was a deficit, this one amounting

Receipts From and Payments to the Public, 1958-65

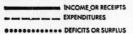

—————— INCOME OR RECEIPTS
— — — — — EXPENDITURES
●●●●●●●●●●●● DEFICITS OR SURPLUS

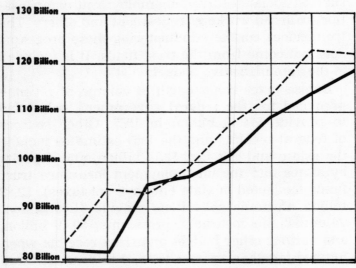

Net: Surplus or Deficit

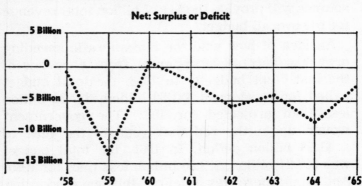

to $2.30 billion. It was the same story in 1963, the budget hitting $109.73 billion, $10 billion less than for 1965, and the deficit amounting to $4.01 billion.

During the 1958-65 period, total budget receipts have increased at an average rate of $5.5 billion annually. Even so, they have not kept pace with the spending because deficits averaging $4.6 billion per year have been shown.

The same sort of trend has existed, quite naturally, in the administrative budget for the same period. In 1958, receipts were set at $68.55 billion, or $24.45 billion less than in 1965. The deficit was $2.81 billion. In 1961, the receipts were $77.65 billion, or $15.35 billion less than for 1965, and the deficit was $3.85 billion. And in 1963, receipts amounted to $86.37 billion, $6.6 billion less than 1965, with a deficit of $6.26 billion being recorded.

During the eight-year period, administrative budget receipts have shown an average annual increase of $3.25 billion, while the average deficit has been $5.46 billion. This has led to periodic requests, which have been granted by Congress, for legislation increasing the national debt limit.

In examining anticipated federal revenues for fiscal 1965, several interesting statistics come to light which point up graphically the unbelievable extent to which federal spending has grown over the years. Here are some examples:

1. Until 1943, no federal administrative budget had ever exceeded in its entirety the $48.5 billion

expected from personal income taxes alone in the 1965 budget. That year the administrative budget, under pressure of World War II spending, soared from $34 billion in 1942 to $79.3 billion.

2. Until fiscal 1942, no administrative budget had ever topped the $25.8 billion projected from corporate income taxes alone in fiscal 1965.

3. In fiscal 1941, the total administrative budget was $13.2 billion, nearly $3 billion lower than the employment tax receipts estimated for 1965.

4. The national debt in fiscal 1941 was $48.9 billion, exceeding for the first time the personal income tax collections anticipated in 1965.

5. The U. S. government spent less money from the time it entered World War I against Germany on April 6, 1917, until hostilities were formally ended on July 2, 1921, than the 1965 budget calls for in personal income taxes from the American people. The declaration of war came late in fiscal 1917 and expenditures in that budget totaled $1.95 billion. The figure rose to $12.66 billion in fiscal 1918 and $18.44 billion in fiscal 1919. With actual fighting ended, 1920 saw outlays of $6.35 billion and they dropped to $5.05 billion for fiscal 1921, which ended two days before peace was officially declared. The total for the period was $44.45 billion, $4.1 billion less than anticipated 1965 personal income tax receipts.

6. The nation's largest budget surplus in history was recorded in fiscal 1948 when receipts surpassed expenditures by $8.419 billion. Amazingly, it was achieved with total administrative income

of $41.4 billion, $56.5 billion less than the 1965 figure, and $7.1 billion below the total due from personal income taxes.

Where It Goes

Where do these billions upon billions of dollars go each year in federal spending? The bureaucrats have left few stones unturned in their search for ways of pouring out the tax funds. The dollars go for national defense; for gifts and low interest loans to foreign countries; for space exploration and research; for farm subsidies to cut production and to pay for storing and handling the resulting surpluses; for forests, fish and wildlife; for regulation of business and construction of highways; for urban renewal and public housing; for public assistance and aid to education; for veterans' benefits and tax collections, and for interest on an ever-growing national debt.

There are two ways of chopping up the budget dollar for a broad understanding of where most of the funds go. One way uses the administrative budget, the other uses the total budget.

A breakdown of the administrative budget for fiscal 1965, for instance, shows this: defense, space and international activities, 62 cents; interest, 11 cents; health, labor and welfare, 6 cents; agriculture, 5 cents; veterans, 5 cents, and all other functions, 11 cents.

When the entire budget is considered, here's the way the dollar breaks down: national defense,

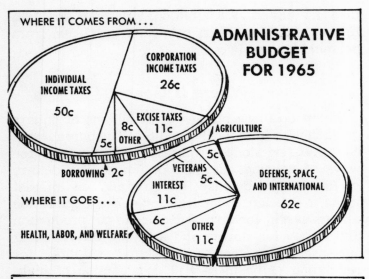

WHERE IT COMES FROM . . .

ADMINISTRATIVE BUDGET FOR 1965

INDIVIDUAL INCOME TAXES 50c

CORPORATION INCOME TAXES 26c

EXCISE TAXES 11c

8c OTHER

5c

BORROWING 2c

WHERE IT GOES . . .

AGRICULTURE

VETERANS 5c

INTEREST 11c

DEFENSE, SPACE, AND INTERNATIONAL 62c

6c

OTHER 11c

HEALTH, LABOR, AND WELFARE

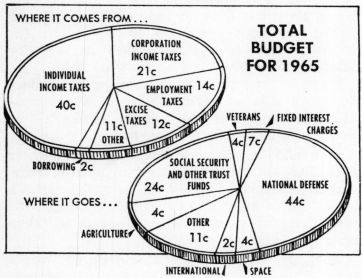

WHERE IT COMES FROM . . .

TOTAL BUDGET FOR 1965

INDIVIDUAL INCOME TAXES 40c

CORPORATION INCOME TAXES 21c

EMPLOYMENT TAXES 14c

EXCISE TAXES 12c

11c OTHER

BORROWING 2c

WHERE IT GOES . . .

VETERANS 4c

FIXED INTEREST CHARGES 7c

SOCIAL SECURITY AND OTHER TRUST FUNDS 24c

NATIONAL DEFENSE 44c

4c

OTHER 11c

2c 4c

AGRICULTURE

INTERNATIONAL

SPACE

116

44 cents; health, labor and welfare (including trust fund payments), 24 cents; interest, 7 cents; agriculture, 4 cents; veterans, 4 cents; space, 4 cents; international activities, 2 cents, and all other functions, 11 cents.

Estimated expenditures by various departments and agencies in 1965 range from a modest $28 million for the executive office of the President to the Defense Department's $51.2 billion for military and $1.19 billion for civil defense. The Treasury Department, saddled with the interest on the national debt, proposes to spend $12.33 billion.

Other expenditures topping the billion-dollar mark include: Department of Agriculture. $5.81 billion; Department of Health, Education and Welfare, $5.85 billion; Veterans Administration, $5.06 billion; National Aeronautics and Space Administration, $4.90 billion; funds appropriated to the President (foreign economic assistance, etc.), $2.5 billion; Atomic Energy Commission, $2.73 billion, and Department of Interior, $1.19 billion.

The administrative budget does not deal solely with estimated receipts and revenues for a given fiscal year. There is the matter of new obligational authority, which embraces what is commonly known in legislative circles as "back door spending." No federal funds can be spent without specific authority from Congress. The intent of this provision is that Congress review the activities of each agency annually and then appropriate needed funds for the coming fiscal year. However, under the "back door spending" policy instituted in the 1930's Congress surrenders this right of review and control in many instances and government costs soar as a result.

The budget, submitted six months before the fiscal year begins, presents a President's recommendations to Congress for amounts of new obligational authority necessary to carry out the program he is proposing. New obligational authority is composed of three kinds of authorizations. The first is appropriations, which authorize agencies to order goods and services, draw the money from the Treasury and pay the bill. The second is contract authorizations, a form of "back door spending." This allows agencies to contract for the purchase of goods and services, but not make expenditures to pay for them. In other words, it is about the same thing as a charge account. After the obligations are incurred, the agency then returns to Congress, presents the bill and gets an appropriation to cover it. The legislators have had no say in the matter until now and the obligations already have been incurred. The third is authorization to expend from debt receipts, another form of "back door spending." It permits agencies to borrow operating funds, usually through the Treasury, contract for their use, and to pay the amounts authorized. Again Congress has waived its right of review and control.

In most cases, new obligational authority

becomes available each year as voted by Congress. In some, such as interest on the national debt, the authority is perpetuated. Only a part of the obligational authority enacted in a given fiscal year is spent in the same year. For instance, appropriations to cover the cost of a new military installation, or development of a new-type aircraft, or building a missile center would be spent over a period of several years because of the time required to prepare designs, conclude contracts and complete production or construction. On the other hand, appropriations for salaries and routine operational expenses of an agency would be used up in the current fiscal year.

Here is the picture on new obligational authority and expenditures estimated for fiscal 1965. Unspent authorizations enacted in prior years amount to $90.4 billion. Of this, $1.3 billion is in authorizations which are expiring. This is deducted from the total. Of the remainder, $61.8 billion is designated for expenditure in later years and $27.4 billion is designed to be spent in 1965.

Now, the President's budget requests new obligational authority of $103.8 billion. Of this, $70.5 billion is to be spent in 1965 and $33.2 billion in future years. When the $27.4 billion in past authorizations is added to the $70.5 billion requested in the new budget, we have the $97.9 billion in the 1965 administrative budget. And, assuming that it is voted by Congress, we add the $33.2 billion from new obligational authority to the $61.8 held over from past authorizations

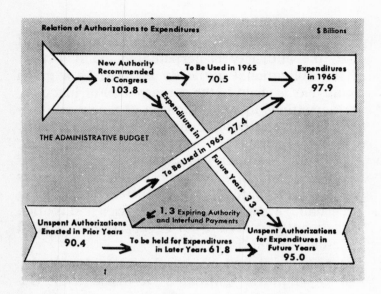

Relation of Authorizations to Expenditures — $ Billions

New Authority Recommended to Congress 103.8 → To Be Used in 1965 70.5 → Expenditures in 1965 97.9

THE ADMINISTRATIVE BUDGET

Expenditures in

To Be Used in 1965 27.4

To Be Used in 1965

Future Years 33.2

Unspent Authorizations Enacted in Prior Years 90.4 → To be held for Expenditures in Later Years 61.8 →

1.3 Expiring Authority and Interfund Payments

Unspent Authorizations for Expenditures in Future Years 95.0

and wind up with $95 billion in unspent authorizations for expenditures in future years. This is a $4.6 billion increase over the figure at the start of the year.

In his budget message to Congress, President Johnson had this comment:

"Obligations incurred by federal agencies under authority provided by the Congress are the forerunners of federal expenditures. Expenditure control, therefore, depends substantially upon careful control of obligations."

This makes it abundantly clear that before there can be any real balanced budgets and any progress toward reduction of the staggering national debt, annual requests for obligational authority must be held substantially below proposed annual expenditures. The American people would be extremely naive to conclude that the proposed 1965 budget is an accurate indicator that federal spending is going to level off or decrease in the future. Actually, the opposite is true because the proposed $103.8 billion in new obligational authority is nearly $6 billion higher than proposed expenditures and, as the President said, these obligations "are the forerunners of federal expenditures."

Plugging The Drain

Enactment of the national dividend plan would provide a five-year cushion on which a sustained program of reducing obligations and expenditures could be carried out. The triple impact of activated investment capital, sharply increased employment because of new plants and products, and overall stimulation of purchasing power by direct dividend payments to the voters would quickly and effectively take up any economic slack which might result from phasing out and eliminating many of the costly, wasteful bureaucratic programs.

More important, however, the national dividend plan would remove all real or imagined need for starting any new welfare state programs. What more effective weapon could be brought into play in President Johnson's proposed "war on poverty?" With every voter sharing directly in up to 50 per cent of the earnings of the nation's corporations and every man, woman and child benefiting both directly and indirectly from the booming, full-employment economy it would create in the technological era, there would be no poverty for the bureaucrats to squander tax funds fighting.

Sweeping economies can be achieved in the operation of our government. Enough of them can be made within the five years required to put the national dividend into full effect to offset the loss of corporate income taxes from the general fund.

Foreign Aid And Foreign Policy

During the last 22 years, the United States Government has poured out nearly $150 billion in foreign aid. Reduced to a more understandable level, this means the taxpayers have been footing the bill for financial assistance in one form or another for most of the nations of the world at the rate of nearly $19 million every day during that long span.

The end of this steady drain on the nation's financial resources is nowhere in sight. There are growing indications that the American people have had enough of the costly program with its attendant waste, mismanagement and questionable overall record of success. And there are signs, too, that members of Congress are beginning to heed the ground swell of opposition by their constituents. This was demonstrated initially when Congress cut President Kennedy's requested aid bill for fiscal 1963 by 20 per cent to a total of $3.9 billion. Then followed a $1.5 billion slash from the Kennedy-Johnson administration's request for fiscal 1964. Even so, the taxpayers still were tagged with a bill for $3 billion.

In spite of its terrific cost to them, few taxpayers are fully familiar with the foreign aid program. Actually, foreign aid is not new to our government. Its real beginning dates back to 1794, during George Washington's second term as President. That year Congress voted $15,000 to help refugees from Haiti. The action came, however, only after a hot controversy over whether it was legal to use American tax funds to help foreigners. Eighteen years later, Congress voted $50,000 to aid victims of an earthquake in Venezuela.

A helping hand in the form of financial assistance was extended on numerous other occasions between the Venezuelan disaster in 1812 and 1941, when foreign aid as we know it today came into being. In each of those earlier instances, the amount of help given was modest when related to the nation's overall wealth. It was motivated by a basic characteristic of the American people to help when tragedy or disaster strikes. The assistance in no way could be construed as harmful to our national fiscal well-being. There was no need to create special bureaus to administer the funds.

It is a different story with the non-stop spending under the modern version of foreign aid. An examination of the record over the last 22 years leaves an impression that the primary requirement for sharing in our largesse is a willingness to accept whatever our bureaucrats dream up to offer. The ideological foundation of the foreign governments being aided obviously has had little to do with qualifying for our generosity. Communist, Socialist, totalitarian, dictatorial, anti-U.S. neutralist pro-U.S. all have benefited. And there have even been instances where when offered aid was rejected, our government has insisted almost indignantly that it be accepted.

How It Started

The vast foreign aid complex of today had its beginning in the World War II Lend-Lease program. Launched in 1941 prior to our entry into the conflict, this was a clear-cut military assistance venture which ended quite successfully with the war in mid-1945. It entailed expenditure of $49.7 billion. Little did anyone, except perhaps the ever-growing core of bureaucrats in Washington, realize that its framework would be adapted for construction of a perpetual motion spending machine.

The new mechanism went into operation soon after the war's end and churned out $14.5 billion in a relief program which was designed to tide the world over during the transition from war to peace. It took three years to find out the program was not working as planned and to shift into another gear. However, one small facet which started during the three-year period did eventually meet with considerable success. It was the military assistance given to Greece and Turkey to help them block a threatened Communist takeover in 1947.

The new gear into which foreign aid spending was thrown in 1948 was the Marshall Plan, named for Gen. George C. Marshall, then Secretary of State. It embraced expenditure of $15.6 billion in economic assistance to put war-torn Europe back on its feet. Measured in terms of European economic and industrial restoration, there can be no question of its success. However, measured in terms of the economic well-being of the United States, there are vast areas for doubt because those modern, technology-blessed industries which were restored with U. S. tax funds now are taking big bites out of both foreign and domestic markets of U. S. industries.

It was after the Communist attack in Korea in 1950 that the aid program's emphasis began shifting from economic to military assistance. By 1952 the ratio was about three-quarters military and one-quarter economic. This "mutual security" period continued into the second term of President Eisenhower, when the non-military spending moved back into the fore.

Since then the stress has been on stimulating economic growth in the underdeveloped areas of the world. This is an extension and expansion of the "Point Four" program of technical assistance to backward nations started by President Truman in 1949. Today, 70 per cent of the spending goes toward this end, although various phases have been given new names such as "Food for Peace" and the "Alliance for Progress." And some new outlets for the spending have been dreamed up, too, such as establishment of the Peace Corps, whose members are sent into the underdeveloped and backward nations to give technical aid.

The overriding aim of the program during most of the post-war period, regardless of whether the spending was for economic or military assistance, has been the containment of Communism. With such a lofty ideal, it has received bipartisan support. And because of this, foreign aid has become the major factor in our foreign policy. Reduced to bare simplicity, it has been used to buy the friendship of most of the other nations of the world under the guise of keeping them from falling into the hands of the Communists.

Proponents of the foreign aid program say it has succeeded. Opponents, who are growing in number with Congressional passage of each new annual appropriation for this purpose, say it has not. All agree it has been a costly burden for the American taxpayers.

Pro And Con

The foreign aid supporters point out that nearly 100 nations have retained their independence with our help and a number of them have been put on the road to self-support. They say, too, that with the exception of Cuba, no country has gone Communist within the last 15 years.

On the other hand, opponents argue that this country has been played for a monumental international financial sucker, with 104 nations having received our financial help during the 18-year post-war period. Many of them have had their requests easily and quickly approved through the simple expediency of pleading that the Communists would take over unless they received financial help. This, of course, fell right into line with the avowed intention of the program — containing Communism.

The big trouble with a foreign policy which calls for buying friendship of other nations is that they do not stay bought for long. Instead, many start practicing international blackmail. This blackmail takes on different forms. In some instances the nations receiving aid will increase their requests, claiming they have been given too little to properly cope with their problems. Others will take our aid and then drift into a so-

128

called "neutralist" position in the ideological cold war between East and West. However, instead of remaining neutral, they often lean toward the Communists on various major international issues. This has the effect of putting our bureaucrats into a state of near-panic and they start pumping out new funds, vigorously defending the flow of aid to the "neutral" against the heated demands by opponents that it be cut off as a retaliatory move.

The government of India is an excellent example of one adroit at the art of international blackmail. Nearly $4 billion in American assistance has been poured into that country. In spite of this, India rarely stands with us on major issues involving this country and Soviet Russia. Yet, when the border dispute between India and Red China, which had smoldered for years, flared into open warfare in late 1962, "neutralist" India turned to us for stepped up assistance to meet the crisis. And we gave it.

Another recognized expert in the use of blackmail and other pressures to obtain our financial aid is Indonesia. The sprawling island nation owes its independence in a large degree to the moral support it received from the United States and Great Britain when it sought to emerge from Dutch colonialism following World War II. Since that time it has received nearly $700 million in U.S. aid designed to assure the political freedom of its people and its overall economic growth. Instead, its government today, headed by

President-Premier Achmed Sukarno, is a rigid, armed pro-Communist dictatorship, bent on the conquest of smaller free nations in that part of the world.

Back in 1962, President Sukarno pleaded an emergency situation in his country and the bureaucrats administering the foreign aid program promptly approved a $17 million loan at negligible interest rates. The following day, testimony before the House Appropriations Subcommittee later revealed, the Indonesian government announced it would spend $20 million to buy three U.S. jet airliners for President Sukarno's private use. This, of course, left our government, the bureaucrats and the aid program in a ridiculous position.

But that isn't all of the story. President Sukarno took a dim view of successful British efforts to create the Federation of Malaysia by linking the Federation of Malaya with North Borneo, Sarawak, Brunei and Singapore. Sukarno has long cast covetous eyes at much of this territory, particularly North Borneo. Additionally, the newly-formed group is strongly anti-Communist, a position Sukarno openly dislikes.

The Indonesian leader's resentment toward the new federation, which came into formal being late in 1963, has been so strong he has embarked on an economic boycott against it. He has deliberately shifted to new channels that portion of Indonesia's trade which formerly went through Malaysia. Normally one-third of Indonesia's trade is conducted through Singapore and Penang, but now Sukarno has the Indonesian shipments go through the markedly less efficient ports and administration of the Philippines and Hong Kong. The result is that he is causing severe damage to Indonesia's economy and effectively negating the benefits and advantages of the foreign aid we and other Western nations have been supplying. Even though he has launched this policy of self-destruction for a dubious political gain, there has been no indication from the bureaucrats that there will be any lessening in the amount of foreign aid we will continue to pour into Indonesia.

'Containing Communism'

A point of grave concern to many Americans is how the bureaucrats in our government have justified foreign aid gifts and loans to Communist countries when the major purpose of the whole program is supposed to be the containment of Communism. They feel that Communism is Communism, or Marxism, no matter what national label it might wear, and, as such, it diametrically opposes and seeks to destroy the free enterprise, capitalistic system upon which our society has been built and is thriving. They can not find one iota of evidence to support the bureaucratic contention that taxing free people to aid a Communist government is beneficial to the preservation of a free society.

131

In spite of their indefensible position, the bureaucrats have dished out quite large sums of free tax dollars to Communist countries. Yugoslavia, for instance, under the tight dictatorial control of Communist Marshal Tito since the end of World War II, has received $2.4 billion in U.S. aid. Poland, a Russian satellite since Communist Joseph Stalin grabbed it from the iron-fisted grip of Nazi Adolf Hitler at the close of the war, has received $500 million. Proponents are able to defend these complete contradictions of the aid program's purpose on the ground that although Yugoslavia is Communist, it is free of Russian control and can defy the Soviet Union and get away with it. Just what this defiance means in terms of benefits to the American taxpayers or to our national security has never been spelled out. Surely even the bureaucrats do not seriously believe for a moment that Yugoslavia could stand up to Russia's military power for more than a brief, fleeting interval in the event of a genuine showdown. And the defense given in Poland's case is even more unrealistic. They say that while Poland's freedom from Russian control is admittedly limited, it is an inspiration to her people and to others behind the Iron Curtain. Just what that means to the American taxpayers and our national security has not been spelled out either.

Another area of the program which galls the average American is the waste, mismanagement and irresponsibility which have come to light in the administration of aid funds. The bureaucrats point to Greece, Israel, Thailand, Japan and the Philippines as evidence of the program's success because they are almost ready to go off the dole after rebuilding their economies with our assistance. But at the same time, opponents point in rebuttal to the mess in South Korea, to South Viet Nam teetering on the verge of complete disaster for more than two years, to Pakistan flirting with Red China, to Brazil on the brink of Communism after $2 billion in aid, and to Argentina, suffering inflationary chaos and under direct military domination after getting $640 million.

Fiscal Irresponsibility

The opponents have some other eye-opening examples, too. For instance, Saudi Arabia is one of the richest little countries in the world with its vast oil resources. Yet, for some reason known only to the bureaucrats, we found it necessary to give about $72 million to King Saud during the last several years. And in South Viet Nam, where military and economic aid has been costing us a million dollars a day for more than two years, a highway project was approved at a cost of $18 million. By the time it was completed, more than $129 million had been poured into the venture. In Panama, approval was given to a new highway and several million dollars had been spent on construction when the shocked American

133

public learned there had been no advance engineering study or planning before the work started. And now look at Panama's attitude toward us.

Supporters of the foreign aid program point out that much of the assistance is in the form of loans, that eventually these funds will be repaid. There is much more to the full picture, however. The loans are long-term, ranging up to 50 years in most instances. The borrowing nation is charged no interest during the first 10 years. For the next 40 years, it is charged three-quarters of one per cent interest. In the meantime, our government, with a constantly climbing national debt limit, is paying $11 billion in interest per year on its obligations, many of which were created by the foreign aid spending. During calendar 1962, the average interest cost to our government for borrowing money was 3.361 per cent. In calendar 1963, this had climbed to an estimated 3.39 per cent. Yet, while we were paying that rate with the one hand, we were lending billions out with the other at no interest for the first 10 years and three - quarters of one per cent for the following 40 years.

This sort of fiscal insanity is apparent in one of the arguments advanced by the bureaucrats in support of foreign aid. They say the program must be continued to prevent a damaging blow to our own economy because 80 per cent of the foreign aid dollars are spent in the United States. A young member of Congress, 30-year-old Rep.

Ed Foreman, a Republican from Odessa, Texas, provided this classic answer on that score:

"The fact is, 100 per cent of the dollars appropriated for foreign aid will ultimately have an effect on the U. S. economy in one of these three ways: For the payment of goods and services shipped free of charge to foreign countries; for the purchase of U. S. gold by foreign nations as a result of the free dollars we have credited to them; or, for speculation.

"A question we might well ask is this: If 80 per cent of the foreign aid dollar is spent in the United States and this expenditure is beneficial to our economy, would there be more prosperity in America if expenditures for the program were doubled or tripled? The answer, of course, is that our own resources would soon be depleted. Our false prosperity would come to an abrupt end, and we would be a bankrupt nation."

How Private Enterprise Can Do It

Even the bitterest foes of foreign aid will concede that an abrupt scrapping of the program is out of the question. The economy of too much of the rest of the world is tied too closely to our generosity. Economic and political chaos would develop quickly and spread around the globe. However, a gradual phasing out of the program with no economic or political ill effects is certainly quite possible with the national dividend plan in force. Free enterprise can accomplish this smoothly, easily and to its own lasting benefit.

The solution is to let private enterprise take over the economic development activities now being carried out by our government. Let investment dollars replace tax dollars. Let these investment funds come from American sources and also from sources within each of the countries being aided. Let them work together in a common partnership whose aim is profit, the creation of more funds for further investment and reinvestment in the growth and development of an ailing economy. Such a program is bound to succeed because private capital would be putting up the money and private capital would be seeking private gain, thereby eliminating bureaucratic red tape, favoritism, patronage, waste, mismanagement and the countless other unnecessary expenses which have come to light in the program over the years.

When a government becomes involved in a foreign venture the possibilities are great that various kinds of entanglements will occur, some minor, others sufficiently serious to even raise the threat of war. On the other hand, when a private individual, company or corporation goes into a foreign land to undertake a joint venture with local capital, it is most unlikely that issues serious enough to affect the good relations between the two governments will arise. When local capital is invested in these ventures, it assures the country in question that from the profits will also come

136

reward to local citizens who put up money and to local labor as well. And this, in turn, will provide reward to the country's overall economy through more jobs, increased buying power and a higher standard of living.

A fine example of how a U. S. corporation has worked successfully with foreign capital in other countries is seen in a plan conceived by Pan American World Airways. In many of the nations in which it operates in Central and South America, Pan American has formed subsidiaries. Each subsidiary owns and operates a domestic air line in its own country. The subsidiaries are jointly owned by private stockholders in each country and Pan American. Their success depends upon the know-how provided by Pan American plus the capital and cooperation of the local stockholders. This participation by local money, management and personnel removes any semblance of foreign exploitation. It also virtually eliminates the possibility of expropriation or similar problems which sometimes ensnare firms totally owned by outside interests.

Phasing Out

If the national dividend plan were put into operation first, it would be possible to phase out the foreign aid program within five or fewer years without Congress having to appropriate an additional dollar beyond the amount set for the fiscal year the dividend goes into effect. Assured by the dividend plan's constitutional amendment setting a tax ceiling on corporate earnings, capital for investment both here and abroad would readily become available. This would mean new plants, mills, factories and other industrial and commercial facilities. The moment construction work started on these projects, a new form of economic assistance would begin for that particular country.

In the meantime, foreign aid through the government could be continuing from funds already in hand, plus the annual appropriation for the year the dividend plan goes into effect, but it would be on a decreasing basis. Since Congress has only five years from the effective date of the amendment to put the plan into full force, it is obvious government expenditures for the bureaucratic follies of the past must be quickly trimmed into line with the loss of all corporate and some personal income tax revenues. Many of the programs will have to be eliminated as quickly as possible, others reduced sharply and then phased out because there will be no further need for them and no tax funds to finance them. Foreign aid is one of many places where the cutbacks can be started immediately and concluded well before the five-year deadline.

As of the close of fiscal 1963 on June 30, our government had in hand $6.9 billion in unobligated, unspent foreign aid funds. This amount alone, according to well-versed members of Congress from both political parties, would be sufficient for the aid program to operate very effectively, and meet all commitments for three years. Even so, Congress appropriated an additional $3 billion for fiscal 1964, ending June 30, thus preserving the $6.9 billion cushion. And President Johnson asked for $3.4 billion for fiscal 1965. Assume that his request is trimmed 20 per cent, the reduction figure used most by Congress on foreign aid bills in the last several years, he still would be provided with $2.7 billion. If the dividend plan could be put into effect in fiscal 1965, then the aid program would have the $2.7 billion plus the $6.9 billion — possibly even more by that time — for a total of at least $9.6 billion to be used in phasing it out over a period of up to five years.

The accumulation of that $6.9 billion in unobligated aid funds raises a point of interesting speculation. It is entirely possible the build-up of this surplus was a strategic maneuver by the bureaucrats to assure perpetuation of the program in the face of a possible future revolt by Congress and its refusal to appropriate any new funds. With this cushion, they could have kept the program functioning for up to three years while they waged an all-out battle to unseat anti-aid members of Congress and elect foreign aid supporters in their places. If this is true, it would be ironic retribution to see the vehicle they had designed for its perpetuity used as the hearse to carry the foreign aid program to its grave.

Farm Program

"It's like trying to suck and blow at the same time."

That's the way Sen. Clinton P. Anderson, New Mexico Democrat, described the U.S. Department of Agriculture's scheme of asking farmers to reduce production, while at the same time offering a higher price for all they could raise on the remaining acreage. The Senator was referring to the unrealistic, futile and extremely costly feed grain program. In the short span of three years, this bureaucratic brainchild has cost the American taxpayers more than $2.5 billion. Yet, the 1963

140

corn crop, one of those it was designed to reduce, was the biggest ever. The new record w a s achieved in spite of huge amounts of acreage held out of production. In the face of this, however, Congress, under pressure from the bureaucrats and thinking in terms of farm votes, approved in mid-1963 a two-year extension of the program which already had clearly proved to be a failure.

While the Senator's biting remarks were aimed specifically at the feed grain phase, they are equally appropriate for the whole farm program, spawned by the New Deal in the 1930's and perpetuated with staggering costs to the taxpayers during the ensuing three decades. Sen. Anderson is qualified to speak critically of the farm program because he tried to administer it from 1945 to 1948 as Secretary of Agriculture under President Truman.

At the farm program's inception, the Department of Agriculture had roughly 18,000 employes. The total grew to 80,000 in 1952 and is above the 100,000 mark today. In 1950, there was one employe in the department for every 125 farmers in the nation. In 1963, there was one employe for every 63 farmers. In 1912, the department operated on an annual budget of $17 million. By 1941 the figure was a whopping $2.5 billion, it climbed to $6.9 billion for fiscal 1964, and President Johnson asked for a $1.1 billion reduction to $5.8 billion for fiscal 1965.

The original functions of the Department of Agriculture were to increase production, expand opportunities and provide for greater use of our resources. With the advent of the New Deal, these functions were broadened to include control of farm production and prices. The aim was to limit output, eliminate surpluses and create higher prices through a program of planned scarcity, thereby boosting the economy of the nation's farmers. Another reason advanced for the laws enacted during that period was that they were needed to protect the family farm, particularly the small farm with the high mortgage.

The only point where the bureaucrats have succeeded in their farm program is in their complete failure. They have been absolutely magnificent in that respect. Not one single proposal they have advanced over the 30 years has achieved its desired result. Farm prices have gone up, but so have the farmers' costs. Production controls have been applied, but unprecedented surpluses have piled up year after year. Billions have been poured into practically every conceivable form of subsidy payments to farmers, but their overall income has failed to keep comparable pace with other segments of the economy. The family farms the program was set up to protect have dropped in number from 6,800,000 units in 1935 to 3,700,000 in 1961, and the decline is continuing.

The non-farm segment of our society has had its fill of the government program almost from the beginning. To them it has meant, quite simply, substantial increases in their food prices, a corresponding hike in their costs of living and a narrowing of the gap between income and out-go, all with no tangible accompanying benefit. On the other hand, at the outset most farmers welcomed the program and its aim of lifting them from the financial ruins of the Depression. Driven by the desperation that gripped the entire nation in that era, the farmers were willing to go along with almost any idea and no price seemed too high to pay. Within a few short years, however, much of the enchantment of the program had worn off. Opposition in the ranks of the farmers began to grow as each new bureaucratic idea for solving the dilemma was tried, failed, and the weight of government controls over the farmers and their farms increased.

In failing to put a ceiling on total parity benefit payments an individual farmer could receive, the bureaucrats doomed the little farmer but established a good thing, in a sense, for the big operator. The latter could afford to combine machinery and manpower for enough production to make the subsidy payments, based on a fair percentage of his output, a profitable proposition. But the little farmer, with his one-horse operation and no machinery, was unable to produce enough on his government acreage allotment to get profitable payments or an adequate support loan to buy the machinery and land he needed. As a result, he mired down in his unprofitable operation and finally gave up completely. That one factor accounts principally for the 50 per cent drop in the number of farm units in this country between 1935 and 1961.

The Ground Swell

The ground swell of opposition by farmers to the agricultural program is taking on new dimensions. No longer is it a minor ebb and flow of individuals voicing personal protests without benefit of group action. Now it is a steady, concerted force growing out of the American Farm Bureau Federation, one of the largest farm organizations in the country. With a membership of 1,600,000 farm families at the end of 1963, the Farm Bureau has set out on a drive to throw off the shackles of government supply-management and return agriculture to the free, competitive market at home and abroad.

As detailed in an earlier chapter, the national wheat referendum in May, 1963, appears to have been the turning point in solidifying farmer opposition to further government involvement in the agricultural production and marketing picture. Soon after the wheat farmers had solidly rejected a comfortable, government-directed peasantry in favor of the opportunities and hazards of t h e competitive market, Editor Paul C. Johnson of **Prairie Farmer** wrote in that magazine:

"I see signs that American farmers have gained both in confidence and independence in the last year. We're beginning to feel that we can compete with farmers anywhere in the world — so we

144

want these trade routes opened wider. We discover that farmers in foreign lands are more afraid of our competition than we are afraid of theirs. We have the land, the equipment and the know-how. We would rather use these freely with a narrow margin of profit than use them sparingly in a program of planned scarcity. One sign of this was the wheat vote last spring when farm people decided to risk drastically lower prices rather than go deeper into a system of government bounty and regulation. Perhaps we are ready to bulldoze out some of the rickety dams we have used for protection for the last 30 years.''

There is good reason to believe that the bureaucrats, in spite of their all-out efforts to put the wheat control program across, sensed impending disaster just prior to the voting and used pressure tactics to save another of their programs which was threatened. Only a few hours before the wheat growers were to go to the polls, the bureaucrats succeeded in ramming through Congress the two-year extension of the feed grain program. Had final action on this measure been delayed until the results of the wheat vote were known, many observers believe members of Congress would have reacted swiftly to the mood of the farmers and turned down the extension.

Grain markets of the nation showed an almost instantaneous response to the wheat farmers' rejection of the new control program. They took on new life and activity. Up to that time the government support price for wheat had been a ceiling as well as a floor. The market price was little more than a reflection of changes in the Commodity Credit Corporation's sales policies. For the first time in years the market price for wheat began to reflect changes in supply and demand.

Similar new life would be injected into the soybean, feed grain and dairy products markets simply by terminating the support price programs. The market prices for all three have ranged for some time at or above the support prices. This clearly indicates the programs could be terminated with little or no adverse effect on producers, provided they were given a little advance notice and Congress also took action to prohibit the dumping of government-held surplus stocks to wreck farmers' prices.

The Not-So-Merry-Go-Round

In setting a $1.1 billion reduction in Department of Agriculture expenditures for fiscal 1965, President Johnson indicated most of the savings would be realized from reduced price support payments. He asked Congress for new programs covering dairy products, cotton, wheat and potatoes.

Cotton is in serious trouble, both on the farms and in the mills, because of excessive price supports. And those excessive supports provide an excellent example of what happens when administrative decision is substituted for the competitive market, when government intervenes in private enterprise. The Agricultural Act of 1958 was designed to permit the Secretary of Agriculture to adjust cotton price supports to realistic, competitive levels. A marked improvement in the cotton situation was noted as a result in the marketing years of 1959 and 1960. Now, if the support price in 1961 and 1962 had been reduced, as was the intent of the law, a further strengthening of cotton's competitive position would have resulted. However, Secretary of Agriculture Freeman did just the opposite. He raised the support price. This ill-considered move immediately brought higher fiber costs to domestic mills, already in a desperately poor competitive position with foreign mills, which buy cotton at lower prices, and with mills using lower cost synthetics. Naturally, domestic consumption dropped sharply. But that isn't all. The higher supports also brought about an increase in the export subsidy from six to eight and one-half cents a pound, a serious reduction in cotton exports, big increases in surplus stocks, and the maximum cut permitted in the national cotton allotment.

Innumerable separate activities are carried out by agencies, bureaus and divisions of the Department of Agriculture under the broad general heading of what the American people call the "farm program." All told these take up 83 pages (telephone directory size) in small print in the annual budget. Of them all, however, the price support program is by far the costliest. It has accounted for roughly one-third of the department's annual budget over a period of several years. In some years the percentage has been even higher.

Under the budget technique used by the bureaucrats, it is difficult enough for the average citizen to even find the price support program figures. Once they're found, it is completely impossible to isolate them and determine the exact cost of the program. They are grouped in the budget under this heading: "Price support, export, supply and related programs and special milk." And all this is under the Commodity Credit Corporation. The "special milk" is surplus milk made available in school lunch programs.

If you stay with the budget long enough, you finally reach this conclusion: In fiscal 1962, the net loss incurred by the price support, export, supply and related programs was $2.636 billion. With the special milk phase thrown in, the loss was $91.67 million higher, or $2.72 billion. Budget estimates for fiscal 1963 placed the loss at $2.735 billion without the milk and $2.734 billion with it, $1.22 million in income showing up. The estimates for fiscal 1964 were identical, a net loss of $2.5 billion with and without the milk.

These losses, of course, are incurred for the most part by selling or giving away various farm commodities for far less money than was paid for them in the form of price support loans or purchases. For instance, in 1962 cost of the commodities was placed at $5.4 billion and the

148

revenue at $2.6 billion; in 1963 cost was estimated at $5.1 billion and revenue at $2.3 billion, and for fiscal 1964, the estimates put the costs at $5.2 billion and the revenue at $2.6 billion.

The Multi-Headed Monster

A real multi-headed monster of the farm program is the huge stockpile of surplus commodities accumulated over the years while the bureaucrats tried futilely to reduce production. Storage and handling costs on these surpluses have been averaging better than a million dollars a day for years. When transportation charges are added, the price tag to the taxpayers goes up approximately another million dollars a day.

In fiscal 1962, storage and handling costs totaled $419.4 million. Transportation, which, incidentally, appears in the budget as "transportation of things," totaled $300.3 million in 1962. This brought the combined total for the year to $719.7 million. In 1963, storage and handling costs were estimated at $392.9 million, transportation at $297.2 million, for a total of $690.1 million. Estimated costs in fiscal 1964 were $344.4 million for storage and handling, $314.1 million for transportation and a total of $658.5 million for the year. Thus we wind up with a three-year bill of $2.1 billion for storage, handling and transporting the very surpluses the Department of Agriculture has been spending a net average of $2.5 billion annually for a long time to prevent.

Supporters of the effort to get the federal government out of supply-management and return agriculture to the competitive market concede that the period of adjustment to market price may be prolonged and painful. A chief reason for their concern is the tremendous surplus of commodities now being held by the government. The mere existence of these subsidized stocks has a depressing effect upon world markets because there is always the possibility that they may be dumped and send prices plummeting.

The surplus stockpile would be even greater were it not for provisions of Public Law 480. Under this measure our government is authorized to sell surplus agricultural commodities for foreign currencies; dispose of commodities for emergency famine relief to friendly peoples; and enter into long-term supply contracts under which sales will be made over periods of up to 10 years and payments received over periods of up to 20 years. Part of the thinking behind PL 480 is that it is cheaper in the long run to dispose of these surpluses at far less than they cost under the price support program than to keep them on hand and pay high storage costs over indefinite periods. However, while this law has helped move some of the surplus — and remove from the public's view some of the failures of the farm program — it has not helped overall world trade in agricultural products. On the contrary, experience has shown that PL 480 and other subsidized sales not only do not build permanent markets but actually hamper private trading.

A Minimum Of Pain

There is no question about the American Farm Bureau Federation and others who favor a return to a free market having the answer to our farm problem. And there is no question about the adjustment period to market prices being painful and probably of considerable duration under existing conditions. However, if the national dividend plan were put into effect simultaneously with the orderly withdrawal of government from farm supply-management, the whole process could be carried out with a minimum of economic pain to the farmers as a group and with maximum economic benefit to the taxpayers as a whole.

The dividend plan's provisions call for its gradual application over a five-year period. The farm program in its present form could be phased out over a similar period. Thus, benefits to the voter-farmer from the dividend plan would be accruing while the price support benefits would be diminishing. However, at the same time, the overall purchasing power of the American people would be increasing from national dividend payments and their attendant stimulation of the total economy. This boosted purchasing power would provide markets and consumption for the farm products which would be seeking their price levels under the tried, tested and realistic law of supply and demand.

It is practically impossible to determine just how much of a saving in federal expenditures could be realized through elimination of the federal supply-management program. If this included only price supports, then the logical anticipated saving would be $2.5 billion, the amount of losses reflected annually for that activity. However, the total would go much higher because price supports are only a part of a many-sided program the bureaucrats have lumped together and dubbed "Farm Income Stabilization And Food for Peace." When all aspects are considered, this grouping accounts for about three-fourths of the total budget of the Department of Agriculture each year.

Actual expenditures for the overall stabilization program, including price supports, for the last several years have been: 1957, $3.430 billion; 1958, $3.284 billion; 1959, $5.297 billion; 1960, $3.602 billion; 1961, $3.801 billion; 1962, $4.591 billion, and 1963, $5.517 billion. The average for that period was $4.217 billion annually. Estimates for fiscal 1964 place expenditures at $4.746 billion, and 1965 at $3.750 billion. If these estimates prove accurate, the average from 1957 through fiscal 1965 would be $4.224 billion.

The potential annual savings are somewhere between the $2.5 billion in price supports and the $4.224 billion average cost of the overall farm income stabilization and Food for Peace program.

No matter what the final saving might be, it obviously will be well worth a determined effort by the American voters to retrieve it from the bureaucrats and restore it to free enterprise, where it can be put back to work in a major, lasting contribution to the real welfare of a free people.

Government

Waste And

Mismanagement

Few Americans have ever heard of Catoosa, Oklahoma, and even fewer live there. Every man, woman and child in the nation should have detailed information about it, however, because tremendous gobs of their tax dollars are being spent to make it an inland port linked to the Gulf of Mexico.

Catoosa is a hamlet on the Verdigris River, not too far from Tulsa. It is 516 miles from the navigable Mississippi River and is tied to that giant among waterways by the Arkansas River, into which the Verdigris empties. The federal

154

funds — estimated to total $1.2 billion by completion — are being used to develop a navigable channel nine feet deep from Catoosa to the junction of the Arkansas and Mississippi.

The Arkansas River is winding and shallow over much of the way and the Army Engineers are finding the going slow and costly. Approximately $150 million had been spent by the end of calendar 1963 constructing finger-like dikes at various bends in the river. Much more probably will have to go for this same purpose. The dikes are designed to catch silt and hold it until it builds up sufficiently to force the river to flow in a regular channel which, with dredging, could be made deep enough to handle the barge traffic hoped for some time in the far future.

Known as the Arkansas River Navigation Project, the venture stands out as a fantastic example of waste and mismanagement of federal tax funds. If this were an isolated instance, it would be tragic enough. However, such ill-considered spending is commonplace both at home and abroad.

For several years our government has been faced with the serious problem of a steady drain on our gold reserves. The foreign aid program, maintenance of military personnel and bases overseas and numerous other factors have combined to create this financially precarious situation. In other words, our spending abroad h a s far exceeded foreign spending in this country.

While it is relatively minor when viewed alone in relation to the multi-billion-dollar spending practices of today, a foreign aid transaction involving Cambodia provides an excellent example of how mismanagement has contributed to our dwindling gold supply. In 1961, our government sent Cambodia $24 million in foreign aid. The Cambodians promptly used $12 million of this money to buy U.S. gold. They continued to partake of our foreign aid generosity until late 1963 when they did an abrupt about-face, informed our government they wanted no more assistance and, as they put it, no more interference, and ended the aid program. Our bureaucrats were shocked beyond belief; a special envoy hurried to Southeast Asia, and unsuccessfully urged them to reconsider and continue taking our gifts. However, they not only stood pat in their refusal, but launched a major "hate the U.S." program both at home and on the international scene, making it quite clear that we have little or no chance of ever regaining any of the assistance given them in the form of loans which were to be repaid. And in early 1964, Russia announced it had given an unspecified amount of military materiel to Cambodia, a final blow to all our efforts to buy a friend and ally in the cold war with Communism. This was emphasized a few weeks later when a Cambodian flier was awarded a medal for shooting down an unarmed American spotter plane near the South Viet Nam border and killing its U.S. Air Force pilot. The Cambodian was flying a U.S. built plane, presumably purchased with foreign aid money.

There's not a taxpayer in this whole broad land who didn't do a deep, bitter slow burn when he learned that part of the foreign aid funds our government gave to Kenya were used to buy extra wives for Kenyan government officials.

About 10 years ago, someone (nobody appears anxious to arise today and take credit for it) conceived the idea of developing an atomic airplane to replace the B-52 bomber. Although many doubts were expressed by qualified sources and the Pentagon's research director fought it from the beginning, the project gained the support of the Joint Atomic Energy Committee of Congress. About five years and $1.2 billion later, Defense Secretary McNamara finally succeeded in killing the project. Countless other millions have been poured down the drain on so-called research and development programs which were sharply attacked as impractical before they were started, but which drew bureaucratic backing and Congressional financial support for varying periods of time.

Out in Kansas, the federal government is pouring $60 million down the drain in construction of a flood control and irrigation dam which many residents of the affected area say is not needed and, even if it were, will not do the job for which it is intended. It is the controversial Glen Elder project in the northern part of the state. Critics say it is being built too far upstream to control

157

floods and will be used to irrigate farm land that is not needed for new crops. In spite of the heavy, two-ply criticism, the Kansas delegation succeeded in ramming the project through Congress as part of a public works appropriations bill totaling better than $5 billion.

Back in 1946 work was started on a huge lake in North Dakota which was to serve as the supply center for an irrigation complex for that arid plains area. The lake was completed 14 years later in 1960, but, ironically, little progress has been made since that time on construction of any irrigation canals. Since the area is primarily agricultural and since the fruits of our farm production already are running out of our national ears, there's little likelihood of any major enthusiasm for construction of the canals being generated in the halls of Congress. So, the taxpayers wind up with a beautiful but useless lake in North Dakota as a monument to the careless, wasteful handling of their public funds.

The Agency That Won't Die

When the bureaucrats dreamed up the Rural Electrification Administration during the 1930's, it was given a specific task. Its sole purpose was to serve as a lending agency to provide federal funds to cooperatives to extend electricity into rural areas. The electricity, in turn, was to be purchased by the cooperatives from federal power installations and sold to the rural customers. While this represented a flagrant intrusion by the federal government into the field of free enterprise, the cooperatives were to use income derived from operation of their individual systems to repay the loans advanced by REA. Legislation provided that the loans should bear interest of only two per cent.

Over the last three decades electricity has been extended into virtually every rural area of the nation and, to all intents and purposes, the REA has fulfilled its assignment. It has been a costly undertaking to the nation's taxpayers because, while the REA has been lending money at two per cent interest, the Treasury, from which it draws its finances, has been paying up to four per cent or more for these same funds. And not only that, the bureaucrats, shaken by the idea of having the agency abolished for the simple reason that it had served its purpose, managed to get authorization for REA to go into the rural telephone business. It still is lending money at two per cent and is draining around $250 million annually from the taxpayers to finance its operations. The net cost of the agency so far as the taxpayers are concerned stands at roughly $3.6 billion.

Up until fiscal 1965, all revenues received by REA from repayment of loans and interest were turned back to the Treasury through the general fund, thus reducing to some degree the net loss of the program each year. Now, however, the bureaucrats have launched an intensive campaign to have the REA increase its volume of loans. And they want Congress to authorize the REA to set up a sort of revolving fund by collecting loan and interest payments and using them for making new loans instead of returning the money to the Treasury. This would have the deceptive effect of appearing as a cut in spending in the administrative budget. Instead of showing an outlay of $250 million for REA, the budget would list a somewhat lower figure, implying that the program was not costing as much as in the past, that a "saving" had been achieved. It of course, would not take into consideration the loss of income to the general fund, although the loss would very definitely be there to the tune of an estimated $150 million or more annually. Adoption of this procedure also would take operation of the agency further away from the control of Congress.

True Babies Of The Welfare State

An estimated 50 million Americans, more than 25 per cent of our total population as of the first of calendar 1964, collect money from the federal government in one form or another, both at home and abroad. This money includes wages and salaries, veterans' pensions, social security payments, retirement payments, farm subsidies, grants of various kinds, unemployment compensation, and numerous other outlays. With that many fingers in the tax fund pie, it is inevitable

160

that there will be all kinds of abuses, waste and mismanagement. And these will increase as the number of persons receiving federal money grows, the amounts paid them grow and the demands for more payments grow.

Our welfare rolls are a national scandal, particularly where aid to dependent children is concerned. At the close of calendar 1963, an estimated eight million Americans were on welfare rolls receiving funds authorized under the Social Security Act of 1935, such as old age assistance, payments to the blind, the destitute, the disabled and to dependent children. The number of recipients has increased more than 30 per cent during the same period. The total cost to federal, state and local governments now is running in excess of $400 million per month, according to best estimates.

Payments have remained fairly constant for the last 10 years for all groups except the dependent children, and therein lies the scandal. When this part of the program was set up, it was designed to assist children under 18 years of age who were fatherless because of death or desertion. In later years it was broadened to include families where fathers are present but unemployed. Now roughly one out of every four families receiving the aid is in this category.

Aid to dependent children accounts for about $120 million of the $400 million total monthly welfare bill. In 1955, there were 2,193,000 recipients. In 1963, the total had grown to 3,912,000.

The average family receiving this form of aid consists of a mother and three children. There are more than 280,000 mothers and children on the rolls in New York City alone.

Much of the enormous increase in the number receiving aid has resulted from the shocking rise in the number of illegitimate children born in this country. Of the roughly 200,000 dependent children in New York City, 40 per cent are illegitimate. About eight out of every 10 illegitimates are in so-called repeater families.

Many of these children are true babies of the welfare state. First, the unwed, pregnant mothers receive medical care and attention at tax-supported clinics and hospitals. Next, they are charity patients in tax-supported hospitals when the babies are born. And, finally, after the babies arrive they soon begin collecting welfare payments to support them.

Truly, the bureaucrats have done their job well by mishandling and abusing the original plan for aiding dependent children. Consider these points:

1. They have been indirectly responsible to a big extent in causing the rate of illegitimate births to rise from 10 per 1,000 unmarried women of child-bearing age prior to World War II to 25 per 1,000 in 1963.

2. They have arranged for all the taxpayers of the nation to share in the expense of supporting these youngsters and their mothers at the price of a heavy percentage of the $120 million monthly cost of helping all dependent children. For

instance, New York City pays $15 million per month caring for dependent children and their mothers. Of this amount, $7 million comes from the federal government in tax funds collected nationwide and about $4 million each from the city and state.

3. They have done absolutely nothing on the federal level to try and correct this shocking situation.

The problem of the illegitimate dependent children is not confined to large metropolitan areas alone. It exists throughout the country. More than half of those involved are non-white, mostly Negro. In some states, particularly in the South, legislation has been proposed — and, in a few instances, enacted — limiting aid payments to only one illegitimate child in a family. These efforts have fallen short of providing a solution, however, because they can be circumvented quite easily. And, too, with the heavy percentage of non-whites involved, they often have become embroiled in controversy over the racial discrimination issue. So, the problem continues to get worse instead of better and the entire nation continues to labor under scandal and a heavy tax burden created by immorality and bureaucracy.

Aid To Expropriation

One of the most fertile fields in government for examples of mismanagement of public funds is in the foreign aid program. And for some unexplained reason, aid to Latin America seems particularly susceptible to this. A case in point is the Alliance for Progress, a vast economic assistance program which was intended to attract private capital and stimulate local investing. Under the plan, Latin America itself would put up 80 per cent of the capital and the remaining 20 per cent would come from the United States, Europe and Japan in long-term, low interest loans. The goal is to finance fundamental economic growth, support social changes "to satisfy the basic needs of the American people for homes, work and land, health and schools," and provide the nucleus for a tremendous spurt in private investment.

The overriding intent of the Alliance, of course, is to block Communism by improving the lot of the common man. However, as is so often the case, it has been a gigantic failure in this respect since it was launched in 1961. Actually, it has been used to advance Socialism in a number of Latin American countries, and instead of stimulating private investment capital, it has seen that capital take flight for safer lands. Ironically, there is every reason to believe the private capital would have remained in the various Latin American countries if the aid funds had not arrived.

Here is what has been happening: Many of the governments have taken the assistance loans and grants and used them to buy out and nationalize private industries. Others have used the funds to balance huge deficits which had been incurred over the years in operation of state-owned industries. Government intrusion into the field of private enterprise, or extension of earlier intrusions, tends to make private investment capital nervous and causes it to seek safer surroundings. This is true, not only of local capital, but also investment capital of U. S. business interests and individuals.

In early 1962, the governor of Rio Grande do Sul, a state in Brazil, seized and nationalized a subsidiary of the International Telephone and Telegraph Co. A couple of months later, the United States approved a $131 million loan to Brazil. One doesn't need a crystal ball to see that if ITT gets any payment from Brazil for the business taken from it, the money would come right out of the U. S. Treasury.

The government of Uruguay is heavily involved in various business ventures, such as electric power, alcohol, railroads, cement, fishing, insurance, hotels, airlines, fuels, meat packing and others. In some instances it has a monopoly, in others it competes with private enterprise. In 1963, it nationalized a cement plant. The money to buy out the private owners came from U. S. assistance funds, which through calendar 1963 totaled around $95 million. These funds have been poured into Uruguay in the face of huge deficits which have accumulated from its unsuccessful efforts to operate its many state-owned businesses.

There are numerous other instances of inexcusable mismanagement of our tax funds in this program. We have loaned and given $700 million to Argentina, which has numerous nationalized industries. Even though the country is wallowing in debt and fiscal chaos, our government okayed a $10.8 million loan right on the heels of a $95 million loan from the World Bank for the Argentine government to expand its activities in the electric power industry.

The Mexican government's involvement in the business and industrial fields is extremely widespread, covering 533 activities ranging from railroads and steel mills to operation of movie theaters. As in the case of Uruguay, it has monopolies in some, is a competitor with private enterprise in others. Much of the funds used by the government to purchase its many enterprises came from loans by the United States and other agencies, such as the World Bank, in which this country is a major participant. A recent $130 million World Bank loan, for instance, was not used for development purposes, for which it had been sought, but went for further government purchases of existing power companies from private owners, thus completing its power monopoly.

Sen. Bourke Hickenlooper, Iowa Republican, successfully offered an amendment to the Foreign Assistance Act of 1962 which specified that countries which confiscate North American property without paying for it can not receive U.S. aid. Its purpose was to provide some assurance that private investment capital would not be stolen outright. Even so, it does not prevent expropriation of such property as long as an agreement is made to pay and it doesn't prevent the seizure of a country's locally-owned private businesses or industries. When local firms are seized, free economies are dealt heavy blows and socialistic state control is advanced. And, as when American-owned firms are taken over, compensation to pay for them usually comes from the U.S. Treasury in assistance funds.

While the Alliance was intended to spur both local and foreign investment capital in Latin America, it has achieved just the opposite. U.S., European and local investors have been withdrawing rather than extending their holdings. A case in point: During fiscal 1963, U.S. assistance to Latin American countries totaled $972 million. During calendar 1962, which covers half of fiscal 1963, best available estimates are that private Latin American capital totaling between $500 million and $1 billion was invested in Europe and the United States.

Negative developments, such as the wrong-way flight of investment capital, make it apparent that someone, somewhere in our government should call a halt in the Alliance for Progress operation until a thorough reappraisal can be made. At present, this country is committed to advancement of $20 billion in outright grants and loans with negligible interest over a 10-year period. Through fiscal 1964, roughly $3 billion of that total had been committed. It would be a national tragedy to have the other $17 billion futilely follow that down the drain.

'Where The Trouble Starts'

When the Senate Independent Offices Appropriations Subcommittee was considering the Federal Communications Commission's fiscal 1964 budget after the House had slashed it $700,000 to $15.8 million, Chairman Warren G. Magnuson, Washington Democrat, said he felt the agency "has too many people." After saying the subcommittee doesn't mind providing more money for good people each year, Sen. Magnuson then added this classic comment: "But the trouble is you put more people into an agency, they have nothing to do, so they make up something and that's where the trouble starts."

The Senator could have had the FCC in mind when he was talking about trouble starting. The agency, which regulates broadcasting along with telephone, telegraph and other common carrier services, has kept the television industry in a state of agitated ferment for years. Many of the industry's problems have resulted from the turnover in FCC chairmen. Every time a new head man is named, he comes from the outside and arrives on the scene with little knowledge about the FCC, its problems or the problems of the industries under its supervision. Most chairmen have swung right into action, however, with heavy criticism of the television industry. Sometimes these chairmen have enlisted the assistance of bureaucrats entrenched within the agency for advice on how to proceed and in other instances they have proceeded strictly on their own. The end result has been the same, however, denunciation of the television industry, new efforts to extend government controls and intrusion, and a generally chaotic condition.

Broadcasting magazine has been bluntly outspoken editorially about the situation and has been pressing for Congressional reforms. An editorial published in October, 1963, had this to say in part:

"A thorough review of the FCC's function and purpose can no longer be postponed — unless the agency is to be ceded the right to make its own laws and choose its methods of enforcing them.

"The recommendations that Chairman E. William Henry put forward last week as a sequel to the Omaha hearing on local television programming are a case in point. Mr. Henry has discovered a function that was never even thought of by the writers of the law that governs broadcasting and presumably the FCC. Mr. Henry says it is the commission's duty to arouse public pressure for better programming even though the public may be perfectly happy with programming as it exists.

"In Mr. Henry's words the 'members of the public are entitled to help. . .in obtaining knowledge of the relevant facts and help in articulating their own needs and those of the community as a whole.' What this means is that Mr. Henry, as presiding officer at an Omaha hearing that turned up little but praise for local television programming, has decided the public is too ignorant to know what is wrong. According to this line of thinking, if the natives aren't restless, the FCC isn't doing its job. . .''

Also in October, 1963, **Broadcasting** said, in part, in an editorial:

"We make the flat charge that the Federal Communications Commission is not serving the public interest, convenience and necessity. These are the counts:

"It is overcommercializing its regulation of broadcasting, to grab headlines and euchre bigger appropriations.

"It is neglecting regulation of telephone, telegraph and other common carrier services which are more important to the consumer economically but which lack the glamor of broadcasting.

"It is squandering taxpayers' funds through 'made work,' such as the inane hearings in Chicago and Omaha on local programming, the harassment of stations on license renewals, unnecessarily prolonged freezes and other contrived devices to force stations to bow to its will.

"It is defying Congressional intent by seeking to arrogate control over, broadcast advertising (which is really rate-making that would transform broadcasting into common carrier status) and by seeking to impose filing fees without legislative authority.

"It is spending so much time — an estimated 80 per cent — on its broadcast crusades which it thinks have publicity value, that many policy determinations are being relegated to staff.

"It is violating its own fairness doctrine (which is of doubtful legality) by demanding on the one hand that licensees determine their public's programming needs and, on the other, ignoring the views of elected representatives of the public, to wit, members of Congress. . ."

The charges the magazine has leveled against the FCC specifically are for the most part equally applicable to other federal agencies and bureaus. This underscores Sen. Magnuson's contention that "you put more people into an agency, they have nothing to do, so they make up something and that's where the trouble starts." In view of the thousands upon thousands of persons who have been put into government agencies over the last quarter of a century, it's amazing that we haven't had even more waste, mismanagement, interference, controls and other "trouble" than we have. Actually, it's remarkable that we have been able to survive as a so-called free country. Never before in all history has a nation been put to such a test.

When President Johnson submitted his fiscal 1965 budget to Congress he made much of a proposed reduction of 1,200 federal civilian employes as an example of thriftiness. When consid-

171

ered in relation to the total number, this cut is about like taking a cup of water out of a five-gallon bucket. The total estimated for 1965 is 2,511,200.

Some bureaucrats will no doubt refer to that figure and say it is only 22,100 above the average annual total since 1942. They would be correct, but they probably would not point out that during World War II the total soared well above three million for three consecutive years, hitting a peak of 3,787,000 in 1945. On the other hand, the total has dropped below two million only once since 1942, having gone to 1,934,000 in 1950. Since then, it has shown a steady climb, reaching 2,490,000 in 1963 and an estimated 2,512,400 in fiscal 1964.

Close examination of the figures shows that the 1,200 total the President mentioned is simply the net saving from a 17,000 cutback effected by the Defense Department. The remainder was gobbled up by increases in other departments. A good example is Health, Education and Welfare, with an increase from 86,000 to 90,730. The total for 1965 represents a net increase of 21,000 over 1963. And the increase between 1963 and 1965 in non-defense jobs amounts to 48,000.

In recent years much criticism has been leveled from many quarters against control and management of news about government agencies through press releases, handouts and other forms of propaganda. There is good reason for such criticism because a total of 8,150 civilians were employed in editorial and information positions by the executive branch of the government,

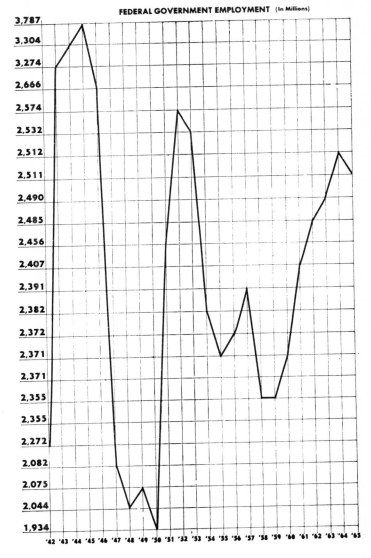

FEDERAL GOVERNMENT EMPLOYMENT (In Millions)

3,787	
3,304	
3,274	
2,666	
2,574	
2,532	
2,512	
2,511	
2,490	
2,485	
2,456	
2,407	
2,391	
2,382	
2,372	
2,371	
2,371	
2,355	
2,355	
2,272	
2,082	
2,075	
2,044	
1,934	

'42 '43 '44 '45 '46 '47 '48 '49 '50 '51 '52 '53 '54 '55 '56 '57 '58 '59 '60 '61 '62 '63 '64 '65

173

according to a survey made by the U.S. Civil Service Commission in October, 1961. That figure no doubt has grown significantly since the survey date because there has been an increase rather than a reduction in such activities.

Positions grouped under the information and editorial category include information and editorial clerk, public information officer and specialist, writer and editor, technical writer and editor, visual information officer and specialist, and foreign information specialist. Persons employed in these positions are concerned with writing, editing and disseminating news stories and releases, the publication of employe periodicals, technical manuals and reports, preparation of exhibits and other visual materials, and dissemination of information in foreign countries for the U.S. Information Agency.

Business Shows The Way

It doesn't make sense that private enterprise, with a small percentage of exceptions, can operate profitably even in the face of mounting tax loads, increasing governmental interference and other such factors which upset long-range planning, while the government, with constantly growing tax receipts, shows deficit after deficit after deficit. This in itself is adequate proof that if sound business practices were applied to government, it could be operated in the black. Enactment of the national dividend plan would go a long way toward bringing such practices into use because the public would be far more unyielding in its demands for efficiency and economy. By sharing directly in the profits of the nation's corporations, the voters would call for an end to government-imposed burdens which reduce profits, bottle up investment capital and stifle steady growth and expansion.

American Telephone and Telegraph Company and General Motors Corporation are two of the world's business giants. Both are products of the free enterprise system. And both operate under tax loads and other forms of control by governments in this and other countries. Let's take a look at the operation of these firms over a period of years as opposed to operation of the federal government during the same time.

Of the two, General Motors would have to be considered by far the more competitive in its overall operations. In the five years from 1958 through 1962, General Motors' operating revenue increased from $9.61 billion to $14.85 billion. It showed an increase every year except from 1960 to 1961. In 1960, revenue was $12.87 billion and it slipped to $11.53 billion in 1961. Meanwhile, net income showed the same pattern, rising from $633.6 million in 1958 to $1.45 billion in 1962. In 1961 it slipped back to $892.8 million after reaching $959 million in 1960.

On the other side of the ledger, General Motors' corporate income taxes rose from $481.8 million in 1958 to $1.47 billion in 1962. Again a dip was shown between 1960 and 1961, income taxes totaling $1.07 billion in 1960 and dropping back to $875.2 million in 1961. Total taxes were $1.44 billion in 1960, $1.24 billion in 1961 and $1.92 billion in 1962. The average number of employes increased from 520,925 to 604,718 in 1962, slipping backwards only in 1961 when the figure was 552,-984.

The significant point in the preceding figures is that General Motors, functioning with the efficiency of free enterprise, was able to show consistent profits during the entire period although fluctuations in the economy mid-way in the five-year span made substantial operational adjustments necessary to maintain a sound basis.

American Telephone and Telegraph showed a steady growth in all five years during the 1958-1962 period. Operating revenue grew from $6.77 billion to $8.98 billion. Net income went up from $981.4 million to $1.43 billion, topping the billion dollar mark in 1959 and continuing upward after that. Employment climbed to 730,000 in 1962. The total tax load kept pace with the revenue and net income patterns, rising from $1.48 billion to $2.10 billion in 1962.

Again, the significant point is that this huge enterprise showed a consistently profitable operation, even though in many instances substantial parts of its operating revenue were under control of governmental rate-making and regulatory agencies.

In the cases of both AT&T and GM, the bulk

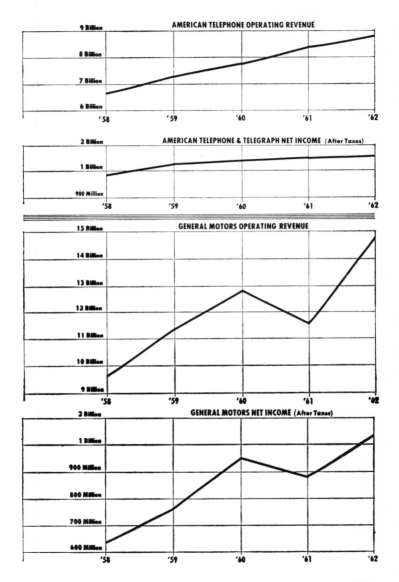

AMERICAN TELEPHONE OPERATING REVENUE

AMERICAN TELEPHONE & TELEGRAPH NET INCOME (After Taxes)

GENERAL MOTORS OPERATING REVENUE

GENERAL MOTORS NET INCOME (After Taxes)

177

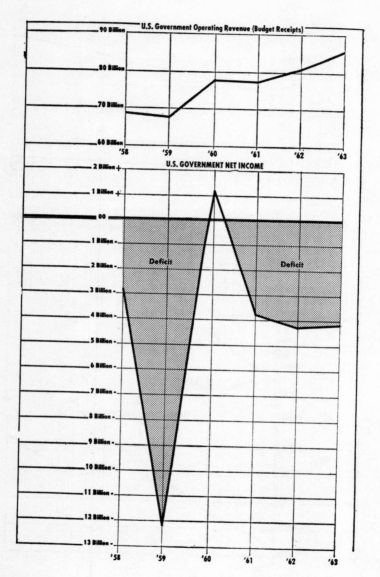

of the net profit was distributed in dividends to the people who had invested their money in the enterprises. Although they were subjected to new tax bites through personal income levies, these funds eventually made their way back into the economy, contributing to its vigor and growth.

What was the federal government doing during the period under examination? Since the government operates on a fiscal year which ends mid-way the calendar year, it will be necessary to consider its administrative budget operations over a six-year span to get an accurate picture in relation to AT&T and GM.

The government's operating revenue (taxes and other receipts) rose sharply between 1958 and 1963, gaining from $68.59 billion to $86.37 billion. However, a drop to $67.91 billion was recorded from 1958 to 1959, and another slight dip from $77.76 billion in 1960 to $77.65 billion in 1961. The number of employes rose from 2.35 million in 1958 and 1959 to 2.49 million in 1963.

All of this generally follows the pattern set by AT&T and GM, operating revenues and number of employes both showing increases. But what about net profits? That's an entirely different story. While AT&T and GM showed substantial profits every year, the government operated in the black only once, showing a surplus of $1.22 billion in 1960. However, the preceding year, it had been in the red for a staggering $12.42 billion and for $2.81 billion the year before that. After 1960, the deficits were $3.85 billion in 1961; $6.37

billion in 1962, and $6.26 billion in 1963. The estimates for 1964 indicate the deficit will be even larger, somewhere around $10 billion.

There is appalling evidence at hand on all sides that waste and unnecessary spending are running rampant in the federal bureaucracy. The late Rep. Clarence Cannon, Missouri Democrat who was chairman of the House Appropriations Committee, estimated publicly, for instance, that there was no real need for spending $8.3 billion of the money Congress authorized for fiscal 1963. This was an off-the-cuff estimate and the figure unquestionably would have been substantially higher had the crusty, thrifty lawmaker been given an opportunity to fine-comb the entire outlay.

No matter what the bureaucrats and political opportunists say, common sense shows there is no justifiable reason for such wasteful mismanagement of the public's tax dollars. A nation which provides the talent to operate its private enterprises on a sound and sane basis certainly can do the same for its federal government. However, the demand for this kind of talent and this kind of operation must come from the voters. And they must first throw off the opiate of the welfare state and its unrealistic something-for-nothing promises to which they have been addicted for the last three decades. The national dividend can provide the cure for this addiction.

War On Poverty

Most thinking people have no quarrel with President Johnson about the aim of his war on poverty in this country. However, his method of conducting that war is open to considerable question.

In his message to Congress outlining his plan of attack, Mr. Johnson made clear he had drawn liberally from the thinking and advice of the hard-core bureaucrats who advocate government intrusion, planning and spending as the panacea for all national ills.

Poverty is not a new problem with which our

government and the Johnson Administration have suddenly been confronted. Governments have wrestled with it for centuries and philosophers and public figures have discussed it for equally as long.

Confucius, the Chinese philosopher (551-479 BC), had this to say about poverty and government: "In a country well-governed, poverty is something to be ashamed of. In a country badly governed, wealth is something to be ashamed of."

Democritus, a philosopher in ancient Greece (460-370 BC), passed along this thought: "Poverty in a democracy is as much to be preferred to what is called prosperity under despots, as freedom is to slavery."

It was Magnus Aurelius Cassiodorus, the Roman historian (490-575 AD), who said: "Poverty is the mother of crime."

The late Eugene O'Neill, the famed American playwright, described poverty as "the most deadly and prevalent of all diseases."

Forty-four years ago — eight years before he was elected to the presidency — Herbert Hoover made this optimistic prediction in a public address: "We shall soon with the help of God be in sight of the day when poverty will be banished from this nation."

In his campaign for President in 1928, Mr. Hoover said: "We in America today are nearer to the final triumph over poverty than ever before in the history of any land."

Mr. Hoover was correct in that remark at the

time he made it. However, Fate decreed that during his administration the Great Depression should envelop the nation, and poverty, destitution and misery should rise to unprecedented proportions. The basic reason for the Depression, of course, was inability of the economy to absorb the free enterprise system's tremendous production without a built-in guarantee of consumer demand and buying power, such as would be provided by the national dividend plan.

It is ironic that the debt-ridden federal bureaucracy we have today is the direct result of the war our government launched on poverty created by the Depression. That was a major war because our national survival was at stake. Those were desperate times and desperate moves were suggested and taken. That fact, probably more than anything else, permitted the bureaucratic dreamers and planners to get into key positions where they have fattened and grown in number and influence ever since.

A quick, surface glance at the nation's apparent prosperity today would lead to the conclusion that the war against poverty which was started during the Depression was an unqualified success. In terms of the overall standard of living of our people, it has been successful, even though, as President Johnson has pointed out, one-fifth of the population lives in an economic straitjacket with incomes of less than $3,000 per year. However, when the financial position of the federal government — which, after all, is the financial position of the American people — is measured in terms of the national debt, the luster of success is dimmed considerably. It becomes quite apparent that the free enterprise system of our capitalistic society, not government spending, is largely responsible for the success we have achieved.

At the close of fiscal 1932, when the first steps in the war on the Depression were taken, the national debt stood at $19.487 billion. At the close of fiscal 1965 it will be $317 billion, if budget estimates prove correct.

Let's examine government spending since 1932 in relation to that of previous periods in our history. Our government operated from 1789 to 1849 with a cumulative surplus of $70 million, but at the close of 1849 the national debt was $63 million. The national debt grew slowly in the period between 1850 and 1899 and stood at $1.437 billion at the turn of the century. From 1900 through fiscal 1931 there were only 12 years in which government deficits were incurred. In two of those years the deficits were less than half a million dollars. However, two war years (1918-1919) brought big deficits and boosted the national debt $22.3 billion to $25.485 billion at the end of fiscal 1919. But it didn't remain there because steady reductions were made in most of the intervening years and it stood at $16.8 billion at the end of 1931.

From 1932 through the estimates for fiscal 1965, there have been only six years in which the government has shown a surplus. The surpluses ranged from a low of $784 million in fiscal 1947 to a high of $8.419 billion the next year. It must be conceded that World War II spending played a big role in the increase in the national debt from $19.487 billion in 1932 to $317 billion in 1965. However, non-war spending has set a high-level pace, too. Five of the six surpluses in the 1932-1965 period have been recorded since fiscal 1946, the last of the big war-time budget years. But the increase in the national debt from 1946 through estimates for fiscal 1965 has been $47.578 billion, even though surpluses totaling $17.129 billion were shown during the same period. In other words, while reductions of $17.129 billion were made, the debt still showed a net gain of $47.578 billion during that time.

From all this we can see that in reality it is not just 20 per cent of the population that is impoverished. It is the entire nation — all the population — insofar as financial obligations are concerned.

What Will They Do Then?

It thus becomes apparent that President Johnson's war on poverty is a minor skirmish when compared with the fight for recovery from the Depression. However, all other features are almost identical, just on a smaller scale.

His campaign is aimed at improving the economic lot of one-fifth of the nation at the

NATIONAL DEBT 1789-65 (In Millions)

FISCAL YEAR	Public debt at end of year		FISCAL YEAR	Public debt at end of year
1789-1849	63		1932	19,487
			1933	22,539
1850-1899	1,437		1934	27,053
1900	1,263			
1901	1,222		1935	28,701
1902	1,178		1936	33,779
1903	1,159		1937	36,425
1904	1,136		1938	37,165
			1939	40,440
1905	1,132			
1906	1,143		1940	42,968
1907	1,147		1941	48,961
1908	1,178		1942	72,422
1909	1,148		1943	136,696
			1944	201,003
1910	1,147			
1911	1,154		1945	258,682
1912	1,194		1946	269,422
1913	1,193		1947	258,286
1914	1,188		1948	252,292
			1949	252,770
1915	1,191			
1916	1,225		1950	257,357
1917	2,976		1951	255,222
1918	12,455		1952	259,105
1919	25,485		1953	266,071
			1954	271,260
1920	24,299			
1921	23,977		1955	274,374
1922	22,963		1956	272,751
1923	22,350		1957	270,527
1924	21,251		1958	276,343
			1959	284,706
1925	20,516			
1926	19,643		1960	286,331
1927	18,512		1961	288,971
1928	17,604		1962	298,201
1929	16,931		1963	305,860
			1964 est	311,800
1930	16,185			
1931	16,801		1965 est	317,000

186

expense of the other four-fifths. The battle plan calls for a new agency, an undetermined number of government employes to staff it and $962.5 million in tax funds to operate it the first year. Actually the new agency — the Office of Economic Opportunities — will not spend all the money and handle all details of the war. It will coordinate the attack by four other agencies already at work in various fields of the program. These include the Agriculture, Justice, Labor, and Health, Education and Welfare Departments. And that adds up to many bureaucratic cooks stirring the broth and inevitable overlaps of functions and duplication of efforts.

This kind of overlap and duplication is typical of a condition which is costing the American people billions of tax dollars each year. Municipal, county and state governments for the most part have been growing in size and cost at a rate proportionate with the federal bureaucracy over the last several decades. Examination of operational structures on all four levels of government shows a staggering amount of overlap and duplication, all under the guise of providing "services" to the people. In most instances, the people could better provide those same services for themselves under the national dividend plan at far less cost and in a manner which would contribute to the economy rather than drain from it in tax dollars.

As outlined, Mr. Johnson's campaign against poverty leaves many unanswered questions. One major phase calls for recruitment of up to 100,000 youths in the 16-21 age bracket in a job corps. They would be placed in camps to work on conservation projects and in special job training centers for a blend of training, basic education and work experience. They would come largely from a backlog of more than one million young men who already have been rejected by the military draft as physically, mentally or psychologically unfit. Half of them would be put to work in groups of 50 to 250 on "special conservation projects to give them education, useful work experience and to enrich the natural resources of the country." The other half would go into job training centers. The decision as to who went where would be based on whether they could benefit more from the work camp or the job training center. As is always true of such programs, the decision would be by bureaucratic decree, rather than individual choice.

These questions naturally come to mind: How would work on conservation projects — such as those carried out by the Civilian Conservation Corps of the 1930's — benefit these youngsters insofar as preparation for jobs in their adult years? Where would they turn for employment at the end of their two-year recruitment periods? What kind of job training will be given those not sent to the conservation camps? Will it be for employment in the automated, technological industries of the new era or will it be the traditional vocational training of the last several decades? Where will the new jobs they're being trained for come from? How can this program possibly create new jobs, except for the bureaucratic administrators and the youths themselves during their period of recruitment? What becomes of the other 900,000 youths in the more than a million draft rejects? And what becomes of those who will join that group in the future? Does this mean indefinite — probably permanent — continuation of the program with expansion from year to year? Does this mean the relatively modest $962.5 million outlined in expenditures for the first year will grow quickly into a multi-billion dollar annual appropriation?

These are just a few of the questions raised by one phase of Mr. Johnson's program. Equally as many others could be posed about his proposed grants of up to 90 per cent for urban and rural community action programs to wipe out pockets of poverty; special grants and loans to help boost the incomes of subsistence farmers; special low interest loans for investments that will provide jobs for low income families or unemployed persons; expansion of an HEW Department program to help train and find jobs for heads of families whose children now receive payments under the aid to dependent children program.

Why Work?

Mr. Johnson is not alone in his concern for the poverty-stricken segment of our population.

The purpose of this book and its proposed national dividend is to bring the fullest possible amount of the fruits of our capitalistic society to the greatest possible number of our citizens; to enable us to move into the automated technology of the future without experiencing a period of widespread unemployment and accompanying poverty and human misery.

Others are thinking along the same lines. And they are making suggestions as to courses of action. In most instances, however, their plans, like the war on poverty, call for greater governmental involvement and more bureaucratic control, rather than utilization of the principles of a free society and a free economy based upon free enterprise.

An example of such plans is one suggested to President Johnson by a group of economists, educators, union leaders and others soon after he had unveiled for Congress his war on poverty campaign. This group, which calls itself the Ad Hoc Committee on the Triple Revolution, proposed that the government pay all Americans an "adequate" income whether or not they work.

The advocates of that plan take the position that automation already has made the industrial productive system "no longer viable" — no longer capable of growth and development — and "the traditional link between jobs and income is being broken." Because of automation, they argue, job-holding as a mechanism for distributing goods and services has broken down and left a huge underclass of "crippled consumers," many of whom live below the poverty line. This, they contend, leaves us confronted with the paradox of managing an economy of abundance on rules devised for an economy of scarcity, and distribution should be divorced from job-holding by "an unqualified commitment to provide every individual and every family with an adequate income as a matter of right."

In theory, the proposal sounds good. The idea of something — particularly an adequate income — for nothing appeals to most humans. But how could such a utopian state possibly be brought about? If no one works, who and what creates the income every person will be guaranteed? How can an economy of any kind be maintained under such conditions?

In submitting the proposal, the group did not spell out what it considered an "adequate annual income." However, since President Johnson has designated those with annual incomes of $3,000 or less for assistance in the war on poverty, it must be assumed that figure would be an absolute minimum. That means it would cost the government some $13.5 billion annually to provide adequate income for 4.5 million unemployed.

It is a basic economic fact that consumption can only be paid for out of production. And that means the 60-65 million job holders would have to foot the bill through increased taxes. This gap between unemployed consumer and employed producer eventually would bring price increases which, in turn, would set off an inflationary spiral of wage and price hikes. The only alternative would be imposition of a permanent program of wage and price controls, such as was in effect during the war years. But, actually, government intervention could not stop there. Who would be willing to work for $60-$65 a week when the government would give them that much without working? If complete economic collapse were to be avoided, the government would be forced to compel people to work. And that, along with the wage and price controls, would just about complete the job of stripping all personal rights, liberties and dignities from the people.

Profits For All From Production

There may be some who will argue that the national dividend proposal actually calls for payments to individuals without requiring work or investment on their part. That is not the case at all. The individual is being paid for voting, technically. But in reality, he is receiving a share of the profits he and other American workers and investors have created through production and sale of goods and services.

The national dividend plan is keyed to production. Without production, there can be no profits. And without profits, there can be no dividend. And without both there can be no continuing consumer demand and buying. On the other hand, both Mr. Johnson's war on poverty plan and the guaranteed income proposal are keyed to non-production. Neither contributes to the economy; both drain from it in government funds.

Adoption of the national dividend plan would eliminate all need for the campaign the President has drafted and for the proposed guaranteed income. Newly-activated investment capital would bring an upsurge in employment in construction of plants and facilities, in the manufacture in existing industries of equipment for the new plants, and in increased economic activity in the areas where the new plants were being built. The demand for workers to staff the plants would eliminate many existing backlogs of unemployment and necessitate the training of new employes by private enterprise — not the government — to meet growing needs of the future. Increased family income in the form of national dividend payments would in itself be a powerful factor in ferreting out and removing the pockets of poverty to which Mr. Johnson has devoted so much attention.

With the national dividend plan operative and private funds doing the job instead of tax monies, there would be no need for a new agency, for duplication of effort by existing agencies, for huge growing annual appropriations, for new increases in the national debt, and for loss of more individual freedom to the federal bureaucracy.

These words from the late Maxwell Anderson, noted American dramatist, in **The Guaranteed Life** are particularly appropriate to the war on poverty and the suggested guaranteed annual income:

"When a government takes over a people's economic life, it becomes absolute, and when it has become absolute it destroys the arts, the minds, the liberties and the meaning of the people it governs."

The key weapon for a realistic and successful war on poverty is at hand in the national dividend for every voter. It only needs to be picked up and put into operation.

Fiscal Soundness

Arnold J. Toynbee, the British historian, has observed that "of 21 notable civilizations, 19 perished not from conquest from without, but from decay from within."

In a decision handed down in 1819, John Marshall, fourth Chief Justice of the U.S., listed several "propositions not to be denied." One was, "That the power to tax involves the power to destroy."

Both of those quotations are appropriate and thought-provoking when applied to the fiscal condition of our country today. Unbridled, wasteful government spending; excessive, incentive-stifling taxation; perennial budget deficits; an enormous and steadily mounting national debt with crushing annual interest payments, all these add up to a form of moral decay capable of destroying any nation. And when the nation occupies the role of prominence we hold today as leaders of the free world, this decay becomes capable of destroying our entire civilization.

The need for fiscal soundness in our federal government is as elementary and basic as the need for it in individuals and in private enterprise. Actually, the need in the federal government is much greater because far more is at stake. If an individual or a business is unable to maintain financial soundness and goes into bankruptcy, relatively few people are hurt. However, when a government becomes bankrupt, financial panic, economic collapse and rampant inflation drag every man, woman and child into a disaster of misery and suffering. And as history has recorded on numerous occasions, the price they often pay for even minor relief is the loss of personal freedom to a strong-arm dictator and a totalitarian form of government.

By the standards which apply to the financial affairs of individuals and private enterprise, our government is dangerously close to bankruptcy today. Many qualified persons feel it already has gone beyond the brink and will never be able to regain genuine financial stability unless major changes are made in fiscal policies and procedures used in the past and continuing today.

At the end of calendar 1963, the national debt stood at $309 billion. President Johson estimated in his administrative budget that it would climb to $317 billion by the end of fiscal 1965. As noted earlier, the annual interest total for fiscal 1965 will be $11.1 billion.

Now, let's look at our gold reserves. At the start of fiscal 1964, we had approximately $15.7 billion in gold, representing a steady drop from $24.6 billion in 1949. Of the $15.7 billion, about $12 billion is required as backing for our currency. This leaves us less than $4 billion with which to meet foreign claims. Those claims were estimated at more than $25 billion at the start of fiscal 1964, the result of an almost uninterrupted string of deficits in our balance of payments since 1950. In only one year between 1950 and 1963 did the value of our exports exceed the value of our imports.

From 1950 through 1957, the unfavorable balance of payments and the accompanying loss in our gold reserves was deliberately planned. Our government felt that this was the only way to increase international monetary reserves and thus restore a free, healthy international trade and payments system after World War II. However, since 1958, the deficits and the drain on our gold reserves have continued at an accelerated pace in spite of efforts to reverse the trend. And, adding to the problem, while the deficits in balance of payments have been averaging about $3.5 billion per year, we have stacked up cumulative federal administrative budget deficits of $40.5 billion, with another of $4.9 billion anticipated in fiscal 1965.

The combination of the budget deficits, the balance of payments deficit and the reduction in our gold reserves has placed us in an extremely precarious financial position. Our currency is backed by $12 billion in gold. However, annual interest payments on the national debt will be less than a billion dollars under that figure in fiscal 1965. And we have less than $4 billion in gold to meet foreign claims totaling $25 billion, or more than six times that amount.

The foreign claims are particularly dangerous to our fiscal security. If the holders of those big dollar balances were to suddenly get together and decide to liquidate, drastic devaluation of the already eroded dollar would be inescapable. And the resulting loss of confidence in our government and our currency at home and abroad would make a shambles of the free world's trade and payments system, as well as of our own economy.

It is not likely that we will face such a crisis, but the possibility is there. And its mere presence serves as a grim warning that we are treading a most dangerous path. Suppose, for instance, several of the countries holding big dollar balances were to undergo political upheavals with control of their governments winding up in the hands of elements friendly to the Soviet bloc. By holding the threat of instant liquidation demands over us, Moscow could call every turn in international negotiations for an indefinite period until we could put our financial affairs in order with a drastic crash program certain to have sweeping disruptive consequences for our domestic economy.

Route To Stability

We must stop our foolish, head-long flight toward fiscal chaos, back-track and take a new course. The national dividend could quickly and effectively lead us along a new route to financial stability, security from possible international threats of pressure and permanent, universal prosperity.

Estimates are the corporation tax will amount to $24 billion in fiscal 1965. If the national dividend were in full effect, this amount would be taken out of the Treasury's general fund and distributed to the voters. This is not all the Treasury would lose, however; it would also have to do without the sum which is now paid in personal income taxes on the dividends received by the stockholders of American corporations. This amount can not be calculated with precision, since stockholders in different income brackets pay varying taxes on the same dividend income, but the best estimate is that it probably amounts to about $4 billion.

Stockholders in corporations would receive the extra $4 billion which they now lose in taxes on their dividends. Most of those who are retired and living on their incomes would undoubtedly spend their share on a better standard of living. Those who are younger and trying to build funds for later retirement would most likely reinvest their shares. Either way, the economy gains greatly, but for the sake of simplicity and conservatism, let us leave those substantial gains out of the calculations that follow immediately and later in this book.

By taking an estimated $28 billion out of the general fund, the national dividend would make the strictest kind of economy mandatory in the operation of our government. At the same time, it would remove the need for ever-increasing federal budgets to provide so-called services to the people because the people would be able to provide for themselves with the dividend funds and the benefits accruing from them.

Although the national dividend would take $24 billion out of the general fund when the plan became fully operational (i.e. after the fifth year), actually the net loss to the government would be considerably less. As explained, the plan would be phased-in over a five-year period. Let's assume that the first year $4.8 billion — one fifth of the $24 billion payable for the purpose — went into the dividend. The second year $9.6 billion would go in; the third, $14.4 billion; the fourth, $19.2 billion and, finally, $24 billion the fifth year. This steady stimulation of the economy coupled with the free flow of investment capital mere adoption of the plan would bring would lead to new plants, products and jobs. With more and

and more spending, there would be more and more tax receipts for the government. As these receipts increased and as the cost of government dropped through elimination of unnecessary expenses, the Treasury would be assured of ample funds to finance the essential services and activities which could not be abolished. And it stands to reason, too, that far better administration of government would result. The voters, as partners sharing in the profits of the nation's corporations, would demand the highest degree of efficiency and economy along with elimination of red tape, bureaucratic controls and interference with the free enterprise system so even greater volumes of profits would be available to the national dividend pool.

With the dividend plan in operation, reduction of the national debt could become a reality instead of a dream for the far away future. As government receipts from personal income taxes increased, it would be possible to maintain federal budgets at a high level, possibly even as high as those of the last few years. This would mean substantial surpluses instead of the perennial deficits, and they could be applied each year toward reducing the principal of the debt. As the debt went down, the costly annual interest load would be trimmed also. Once the debt reached a reasonably sane level along with the annual outlay for interest, the reduction rate could be slowed, if it appeared to be in the national interest, and further cuts in personal income tax rates would be possible.

With industry spurred to new peaks of productivity and profits by the double impact of the national dividend's feed-back into the economy and the marvels of the technological age, our serious balance of payments problem could be solved. In the first place, our products could become far more competitive in the export markets as efficiency of operation and intensity of competition joined to lower costs and prices. This is one of our major problems today. Our products are running into tougher and tougher competition abroad. Higher costs for labor and materials together with obsolescence of many of our plants and factories have combined to price much of our production out of formerly substantial foreign markets. However, with investment capital anxious and willing to go to work, the problem of new machinery could be easily overcome. Additionally, the national dividend in action would halt the flow of U.S. investment capital overseas and result in much foreign capital coming in to participate in the economic growth and expansion and share in the profits.

An elderly friend of mine with a most active mind observed when President Johnson signed the 1964 income tax reduction bill that the $11 billion plus cut should have caused the American people to dance in the streets in view of the overall tax burden they bear. But, he continued, there was no dancing and there was no universal feeling of elation because the people obviously realized that since the tax cut was not accompanied by a proportionate reduction in government spending, it is possible that the rate will have to be restored and perhaps raised. Under the national dividend, the goal of the 1964 income tax cut — stimulation of the economy and reduction of unemployment — could be achieved quicker, more effectively and with permanence. And there would be no haunting, depressing fear of restoration of tax cuts or possible increases.

One does not have to be an economics expert to see that something must be done to shore up and rebuild our financial stability. Economic collapse and chaos are inevitable — maybe not next year, or the next or within 10 years, but, eventually, inevitable — unless corrective steps are taken. The national dividend can perform that service for our country and our people. Admittedly, it is a bold and radical idea. But it will work because it is based upon preservation of individual liberty, perpetuation of free enterprise, decentralization of government and democratic use of the nation's wealth and talents to improve "the life, liberty and pursuit of happiness" of "ourselves and our posterity."

Tax Reduction

When President Johnson signed the $11.5 billion income tax reduction bill in late February, 1964, the basic machinery was set in motion to provide the nation's economy with an estimated $30 billion a year in new spending. That's the conclusion of the President's Council of Economic Advisers as to the economic chain-reaction the tax cut will set off.

Applying the same calculations the council used on the tax cut, the national dividend for every voter would provide more than twice that much in new spending per year, once it became fully operational.

The economists' estimates are based on solid ground, if the experience of the Austrian government with four tax cuts since 1954 can be used as a guide. And, apparently, there is no reason why it can not.

First, let's examine the reasoning behind the tax cut, then check the record on Austria, and, finally, compare the national dividend's potential economic impact with that of the tax reduction.

The economists estimate that the after-tax income of the American people will be $9 billion a year higher than under the old rates. And they estimate corporations' after-tax profits will be $2.3 billion higher. With past dividend payment practices as a yardstick, they estimate the increase to stockholders from the boosted profits will come to at least $1 billion. This, when added to the earlier $9 billion, would increase consumer spending potential by roughly $10 billion.

Of the $10 billion in potential, an estimated $9.3 billion actually will be spent. That's the spending pace — 93 cents out of every dollar — that the American people have established in recent years.

When that tremendous spending increase hits our economic structure, it is certain to bring a big gain in production of consumer goods. This will mean new jobs, more people at work, higher payrolls, higher profits and boosts in farm, professional and service incomes. Like the ever-widening circle of ripples caused when a pebble is tossed into a pool, these gains in production, profits, employment and payrolls would, in the words of the Council of Economic Advisers, "generate still further increases in spending and incomes."

While the council uses a complicated economic theory to explain the spending chain-reaction, the economists suggest that a reasonably accurate result can be obtained simply by multiplying the original amount put into the economy by two. In this case, the $9.3 billion spending potential would be doubled to arrive at a total of $18.6 billion, which they estimate consumer spending would increase the total economy.

The $9.3 billion pebble tossed into the economic pool will cause further ripples in the form of increased capital investments in plants and equipment. Spending on inventories also will increase. And, significantly, the revenues of state, county and community governments will be boosted by the economic stimulation. They, in turn, will be able to spend more on schools, roads, streets, sewers and numerous other services and facilities.

All of these additional factors, the Council of Economic Advisers estimates, will probably total $5 billion to $7 billion in further spending. And, applying the simple plan of doubling the amount of spending, we find another $10 billion to $14 billion added to the economy. That brings the overall total, according to the council's projections, to more than $30 billion.

The soundness of this economic reasoning has been proved four times in Austria since 1954. Income tax rates have been slashed that many times, the economy has made astonishing gains and the government's tax receipts have almost tripled.

The tax cuts in Austria have been quite substantial in each instance. As a result, the rates for low to medium income families now are more than 50 per cent below the pre-1954 levels.

The first cut went into effect on Jan. 1, 1954, reducing, for example, the tax of a couple earning $3,600 per year from $1,453.44 to $1,128.96. T h e government's tax collections in 1955 jumped 12.4 per cent over the total for 1954. And, reflecting the nation's economic growth, the gross national product soared 14.7 per cent.

On Jan. 1, 1955, the next cut became effective. It reduced the tax of the couple with $3,600 annual income from $1,128.96 to $987.44. This meant a $466 reduction from the pre-1954 rate. It also meant an 8.7 per cent increase in government tax collections in 1956 and a 10.1 per cent increase in the gross national product.

The third cut went into effect on Jan. 1, 1958. It dropped the $3,600 a year couple's payment to $843.92, or $609.52 less than prior to 1954. This time tax collections increased 6.8 per cent over the preceding year and the gross national product was up 6.2 per cent.

The fourth tax cut was put into effect on July 1, 1962, and final figures on its effect were not available when this book was published. However, the thriving economy of that country indicated that both tax collections and the gross national product were on their way toward new increases. The latest tax cut reduced the amount paid by the couple earning $3,600 to about $800 per year, or $653 less than prior to 1954.

The Rolling Snowball

Now let's look at the national dividend's potential impact on our economy. Using $4.8 billion as the amount which would go into dividend payments the first of the five years needed to get it into full operation, this is how much the after-tax income of the American people will be increased. This money, you will recall, would not be subject to personal income taxes. The American people spend 93 cents of every dollar of income, so $4.5 billion would be spent. And, still using the economists' theory, this would generate another $4.5 billion in increased spending and income, bringing the total increase in the economy to $9 billion.

This $9 billion would spur capital investments, inventory spending, and state, county and municipal government capital spending by roughly $3.1 billion, which in turn is doubled. Thus we find a $15.2 billion increase in the total economy — coincidentally, almost half the total estimated from the $11.5 billion tax cut — the first year of the national dividend. This would rise proportionately each year until in full effect the fifth year.

In full force, the national dividend would have a tremendous impact when we use $24 billion as the amount to go into the fund. Spending would hit $22.3 billion, which would double to $44.6 billion. Capital investments, inventories and capital spending by government below the federal level would be $15.6 billion, or $31.2 billion when doubled. The total increase in the economy would be $75.8 billion.

Actually, the total increase would be greater than the $75.8 billion because the gains in after-tax income from increased dividend payments by corporations have not been taken into consideration in these calculations. Under the national dividend plan, stockholders would not be required to pay federal income tax on their dividend payments from corporations. These payments, of course, would increase as profits grew and would make a substantial addition to the income and spending potential of thousands upon thousands of American citizens. However, for the purpose of simplicity, no attempt has been made to incorporate this additional income into the projected impact of the national dividend on the total economy.

President Johnson told Congress that the $11.5 billion tax cut would result in year after year increases of $35-$40 billion in the gross national product, $25-$30 billion in consumption and $5-$7 billion in profits.

Using the President's formula — and again making no allowance for corporate dividend payments free of personal income taxes — the national dividend would bring minimum increases year after year of $70-$80 billion in the gross national product, $50-$60 billion in consumption, and $10-$14 billion in profits.

An economy so well-grounded as to assure perpetual growth and expansion would never be subjected to nervous fears of recession or depression. Danger of over-production simply would not exist because the constant feed-back of spending capital would keep domestic consumer demand on a steadily growing plane. And the potential demand for consumer goods in foreign markets is limitless. These continuing demands would enable the economy to adequately meet the demands of a growing domestic population for more and more jobs.

The compelling advantage of the kind of spending the national dividend would provide for our economy over the spending for public works, area redevelopment projects, farm subsidies and what-not advocated by the bureaucrats is quite simple. It is creative spending generated by private enterprise. The other is non-creative spending generated by tax dollars. Under the dividend plan the spending would stimulate the economy and, as a by-product, actually increase government revenues. That advocated by the bureaucrats would provide some stimulation to the economy by increasing circulation of money, but it would not create new dollars. Instead, it would increase the national debt and its interest expenses and further impair the economy by taking potential investment capital from the channels of free enterprise.

Under the capitalistic system, individuals own and manage the principal resources and the productive facilities of the nation. This ownership is the source of independence; it is an essential right which provides incentive and inspiration to the individual. The national dividend for every voter would keep that right firmly within the grasp of the people and out of the hands of an all-powerful central bureaucracy.

Voter Participation

The accomplishments of the capitalistic free enterprise system during the last century have been nothing short of amazing. To review some of them:

The real wages of American workers (wages in relation to prices) have increased several times over. The share of the national income paid out in wages and salaries has doubled. The Gross National Product has soared above the $600 billion mark. The hours of work for the average employe have been reduced from about 70 to 40 per week.

Jobs have been provided for more than 70 million persons.

There is absolutely nothing fundamentally wrong about a system that can do such things for its people. It has its weaknesses, yes. We still have our ups and downs of prices and jobs. We still have poverty and sub-standard housing. However, the accomplishments of the system far overshadow its weaknesses. We should always be ready and willing to look for a solution to those weaknesses, but in choosing one, let us not forget to keep the basic concepts of free enterprise.

Because it is a plan which will provide both for the continued incentive and protection of the capitalist and, simultaneously, provide for the ordinary citizen to share in the benefits of a technological age, the national dividend for every voter would help to eliminate some of our present weaknesses and proceed to add some astonishingly great chapters of productivity and progress in the future.

The national dividend plan, close examination will show, revolves around the basic assumption that under a social and economic system that assures individual freedom, there will be extra reward for extra effort. It is a system that will always use its human and natural resources to the best advantage, both for the individual and the state.

The national dividend plan will, of a certainty, spur production and provide for a share in the benefits. Under this proposal we can continue to

213

progress as we have in the past, but at an accelerated rate and on a sounder financial basis. Within a few short years we can look forward to more and better jobs, improved working conditions, longer vacations, higher personal incomes, better schools, better food, and last — but by no means least — more security. And we can do it without further devaluation of the dollar. Actually, we can do it and restore the strength of the dollar.

The large majority of the people in the world today are not against free enterprise. A great many of them fail to understand it, and those condemning it invariably offer a plan which basically would destroy the foundations upon which our success is built. As we have seen over the last three decades, all too often a plan is offered which calls in the federal government to subsidize. If we are to survive, we must be honest enough with ourselves to acknowledge that at best this sort of remedy can be only temporary. And the agency or bureau set up to administer the temporary remedy usually becomes permanent, thus, in the long run, adding to the problem instead of solving it. We must provide a permanent solution, and this means solving our problems without the federal dole and bureaucratic interference and controls.

The relationship between employe and management is equally applicable to the relationship between the voter and government.

As long as the voters have confidence in their

government, the people will stay bonded together in common purpose. Such confidence can be inspired only by greater participation on the part of the voter in government. The national dividend for every voter will provide such participation and create such confidence.

Satisfaction In Participation

Surveys, polls and studies have shown that, more than anything else, the modern worker or employe wants a satisfying job — the psychological security that comes from good work, the recognition of it and the understanding that his fellow workers feel the same way.

For the most part, the worker sincerely wants to be a real and productive part of the company which employs him. By the same token, he wants to be a real and productive part of the nation and the world. He has a complex ambition to contribute to the good of his company, his country and to all mankind. This facet of human nature is too frequently overlooked in this cynical age. He expects, however, and rightly so, a fair reward for his contribution.

Half a century ago, and before that, people had to work hard to live. There was an affinity between living and work — a union between the worker and the work done. Then we established the production line. The old, healthful way of self-expression was replaced by frustration. A conflict developed. It is a conflict between the freedom of expression which American voters enjoy in their private and political life and the comparatively autocratic life which we find in modern industry.

Naturally, such a conflict creates a problem. The problem increases as the population rises because the conflict becomes greater. If confidence in government wanes over a sustained period, what is to stop a frustrated people from undermining, rather than cooperating with, government?

The only answer is greater participation in government by the people, i.e. the voter.

Private industry has found that where the basic principle of participation has been carefully followed and where management has actually wanted and sought the participation of workers, the results have been most encouraging. Participation in management by the employe has created confidence and confidence has spawned increased productivity. Increased production and more profits have resulted in self-confidence on the part of the worker, and the whole idea has eliminated frustration.

Participation in national affairs in this technological age is as vitally important to the average man and woman as participation in the affairs of private enterprise and those of their own community. More than ever before, the voters of the United States are eager and anxious to participate in government.

Now there are many who will say, if that is

216

true, why don't more of our citizens exercise their franchise and go to the polls? The answer is, many of them feel that their one little vote is not important, one way or the other. A share in the national dividend will change this feeling and give them a personal incentive to vote. The dividend will be distributed only among those citizens who vote in the national general elections. The voter who neglects to cast his ballot simply will not get his share of the national dividend. He then would have a two-year wait until the next national general election before he could vote and again become eligible for his share.

It goes without saying that the voter who exercises his franchise and receives his dividend will automatically take a keener interest in the men he helps put into office. After all, the size of his national dividend is going to depend upon the manner in which those men he helps elect handle national affairs.

The wonders of participation would be revealed, as never before, by the national dividend plan.

It would force every political officeholder to put his department on a sound basis and keep his costs to a minimum. If he fails, his ineffectiveness will be reflected to the "stockholders," the American voters. Stockholders act quickly when dividends decrease. So would voters.

You — as a voter — can be a vital force in the battle for good government and the distribution of a fair share of the nation's corporate wealth to those who are responsible for that wealth. Your

Congressman, your Senators welcome your views as guidance in their struggles with the increasingly complex problems of government.

Active voter participation could accomplish many good things. It could prevent further abridgement of the economic liberties of the American people; prevent concentration of excess power in the hands of politicians, labor, industry or any special interest group; prevent federal bankruptcy; prevent fraudulent, false voting, and eliminate government waste and mismanagement, just to name a few.

The Great Chance

The problem our nation faces today is two-fold: (1) How to restore free enterprise and initiative and keep the inefficiency of bureaucracy from laying waste the efforts of creative wealth, and (2) simultaneously, how to spread and promote the general welfare so that all of the people share in the benefits and profits of this great technological age.

We have a chance now to perfect a great state of civilization. We can achieve this perfection only by curing our own evils first. Then we will be in a position to look into the matter of aiding the remainder of civilization. Unless there is first a return to monetary and economic stability, there will certainly follow failure of our so-called "righteous causes" due to the collapse of our financial structure. History has always borne out this theory. Let us study those past trends and act now to leave the ownership of property in private hands, but let us also encourage that property to produce for all the people of the land.

When we examine the annual reports of the nation's corporations, such as American Telephone and Telegraph and General Motors, and note the efficient, profitable management they have enjoyed, the disparity between the ability of those running our government and those in private enterprise is inescapable. If we could only elect such talent to public office in appreciable numbers, you may be sure operation of government would be efficient and profitable. Couple this with the distribution of dividends to every voter and most of our internal problems would be over, our freedoms would be restored and human dignity would be attained by all men and women of all classes, colors and creeds.

It is this necessity for the democratization of capitalism which we must fulfill. But in doing so, we must find a way which, at the same time, will restore individual freedom, free enterprise and a sound government operation. The national dividend for every voter will achieve these aims.

Free Enterprise
And Free Voter

The American free economy is without question one of the most important factors in the struggle today between the Free World and the Communist World. Nothing must be left undone to preserve that freedom.

Our economy is going to be put to severe tests in the years ahead as the free enterprise system, from which it draws its strength, copes with the many problems certain to arise as more and more technological developments are brought into productive use. Continued full employment is an absolute necessity for a strong and vigorous

220

economy, and this is the area where the free enterprise system will meet its most formidable challenge.

While the challenge will be great, it can be met in such a way that our economy can be preserved and made even freer. All this is possible under the national dividend for every voter plan.

For the free enterprise system to successfully face up to the problem of maintaining full employment, its introduction of the marvels of technology into present production systems must be geared to an assured, steady flow of investment capital and a constantly rising consumer buying potential. It is essential that this investment capital be creative capital, whose sole purpose is to build new plants, produce new products and earn more profits. It must come from private enterprise. It can not be government tax dollars if creative growth is to be achieved.

As the preceding chapters of this book have carefully detailed, the national dividend will assure the steady flow of private investment capital and the constantly rising consumer spending potential our economy must have. With the added feature of greater participation in government by the voters, it would put immediate and permanent brakes on further encroachment by the federal bureaucracy into the personal freedom and rights of the citizens. It also would result in restoration of many of those liberties which already have been chipped away in recent decades.

221

By adopting the national dividend plan, we can make it easier for us to win the battle with the Communist World. We could show the people of the world, and particularly those under Communist rule, that all the people of the United States really own this country, that they not only have the right to vote, but also are paid to enjoy that right. That would end once and forever the ideological war, because the Communist governments could never afford to pay their citizens and it would soon become obvious which type of government was better.

In his economic report to Congress in January, 1964, President Johnson outlined the nation's economic challenge in the future. He said we seek a free and growing economy which:

1. "Offers productive employment to all who are willing and able to work." The national dividend plan will provide the means for doing this.

2. "Operates at the full potential of our human and material resources." The national dividend will make this possible.

3. "Encourages free enterprise, innovation, and competition by citizens in all walks of life." This is a basic fundamental of the national dividend plan.

4. "Avoids setbacks from recession or inflation." The national dividend will assure this.

5. "Generates steady and rapid growth in productivity — the ultimate source of higher living standards — while providing the new skills and

jobs needed for displaced workers." The ability to do this is one of the strongest features of the national dividend plan.

6. "Meets ever more fully the needs and preferences of our citizens, as freely expressd in the market place and in the halls of governments." The national dividend guarantees this.

7. "Provides increasing leisure, and satisfying ways to use the time, to those who wish it." The national dividend and the technological revolution will walk hand in hand in providing this.

8. "Safeguards the security of the nation and the free world by assisting efficiently the economic development and political independence of the less developed countries." What free enterprise can do in this country under the national dividend plan, it can do for other countries of the Free World with its vastly enlarged investment capital.

9. "Promotes mutually advantageous trade with other countries, and progressively reduces barriers to international competition." Booming production spurred by the national dividend and the technological marvels would bring the products of our free enterprise system within the reach of the people of every country in the world.

10. "Earns enough in free international transactions to balance our external payments and yet meet our world responsibilities." The answer to this is the same as for Item 9 above.

11. "Distributes fairly the fruits of economic

growth among consumers and producers, workers and employers." Another basic fundamental of the national dividend.

12. "Moves steadily toward the American dream of equality of opportunity for all citizens — regardless of race, religion, sex, or residence, regardless of social and economic status at birth." What better way than through the national dividend?

13. "Permits every American to produce and to earn to the full measure of his basic capacities.' The national dividend not only permits it, but also encourages it.

14. "Eliminates, with the compassion and foresight of which a free and abundant economy is capable, avoidable suffering and insecurity from the lives of our citizens." This, together with the restoration and preservation of human rights, liberties and dignity, also is a basic fundamental of the national dividend.

Forward Into Destiny

"These aspirations are not easy to fulfill," the President told Congress, "but neither are they beyond our powers."

Under existing policies and procedures, attainment of these goals would be slow and laborious. Perhaps all would never be attained. Yet, under the national dividend, all appear within relatively easy reach, particularly when viewed in relation

224

to the stimulus the technological revolution is going to provide.

The national dividend will democratize capitalism. It will take advantage of free men's total energy. It will combine this energy with the modern tools of automation so that the profits of a smoothly running national economy will be split among its stockholders — the voters.

The ultimate solution to the problem of making our capitalistic society work to perfection must come from the individual, not the state. By limiting the role of the state in the economy and, simultaneously, equalizing or democratizing capitalism, we will have achieved the announced constructive goals of Marxism. But we will have eliminated the hatred which drove Marx to write **Das Kapital,** the one book that has affected so many millions of lives over the last century.

What we must do is simple: Improve our present system by incorporating in it the appeals of Communism and at the same time restoring those necessary elements of free enterprise which have proven so successful.

If we can do this by calling on all segments of the population — business and labor, farm and professional, men and women — we will be on our way to achieving that goal.

If we add to this the scientific and engineering advances of the technological revolution, particularly those fields of automation and others in which this nation has unquestioned leadership, we cannot help but pull far ahead in our struggle to preserve the free way of life.

Under the national dividend for every voter, politicians would have to do a business-like, honest, thorough job, or the stockholders in the mighty enterprise of government, the voters, would throw them out of office.

The individual voter also must earn his keep under the national dividend plan. He must vote in a national election or he will not be eligible for his dividend which will come from the fruits of free enterprise.

This feature of the national dividend plan would go a long way towards ending the voter apathy existing throughout the United States. So widespread has been this indifference towards voting that it has been described as a "national embarrassment."

Once we put our own house in order through the national dividend for every voter, then it will be obvious to the remainder of the world that we have the better system.

There is one way to do that — an amendment to the Constitution of the United States.

An amendment created prohibition. And an amendment ended prohibition.

An amendment created the income tax. And now an amendment is needed to curb the abuses that have crept into this tax and, at the same time, give to the voter an equal share in his rightful heritage.

Not until voter responsibility, authority and

reward are linked together will we be able to make the economy work at its peak efficiency. And not until we achieve peak efficiency will we vault forward into the destiny that is surely ours.

THE NATIONAL DIVIDEND
Where The Money Will Come From
(In Billions of Dollars)

	Source	1st Yr.	2nd Yr.	3rd Yr.	4th Yr.	5th Yr.
Savings In Foreign Aid	Note 1 Chap. 7		3.00	3.00	3.00	3.00
Savings In Farm Program	Note 2 Chap. 8		3.50	3.50	3.50	3.50
Savings In Defense Department	Note 3 Chap. 5	3.00	3.00	3.00	3.00	3.00
Elimination of Waste, Unnecessary Public Works, Etc.	Note 4 Chap. 9	8.30	8.30	8.30	8.30	8.30
Savings In Cost of Government As Result of Cuts In Spending	Note 5	.25	.50	1.00	2.00	3.00
Gain In Corporate Tax Revenue As Result of Increased Profits	Note 6 Chap. 12	1.25	2.50	3.75	5.00	6.25
Total Potential Savings Plus Gain In Tax Revenue From Increased Profits		12.50	20.80	22.55	24.80	27.05
Funds Needed for National Dividend Annual Payments		4.80	9.60	14.40	19.20	24.00
Potential Net Savings In Excess Of National Dividend Needs		7.70	11.20	8.15	5.60	3.05

THE NATIONAL DIVIDEND
Where The Money Will Come From
(In Billions of Dollars)

CUMULATIVE SAVINGS OVER 5-YEAR PHASE-IN PERIOD

Potential Net Savings In Excess Of National Dividend Needs	7.70	11.20	8.15	5.60	3.05
Carry Over In Potential Net Savings From Prior Year		7.70	18.90	27.05	32.65
Potential Net Savings In Excess Of Dividend Needs With Annual Carry Over	7.70	18.90	27.05	32.65	35.70

NOTE 1—Based on recent annual appropriations. Backlog of $6.9 billion in unobligated funds available for phase-out program.

NOTE 2—Based on average cost of price supports and overall farm stabilization and Food for Peace program. First year would cushion termination of program.

NOTE 3—Based on Defense Secretary McNamara's estimate to late President John F. Kennedy.

NOTE 4—Based on late Rep. Clarence Cannon's estimate of unnecessary appropriations for fiscal 1963.

NOTE 5—Based on conservative estimate of reduction in number of employes and agencies no longer needed.

NOTE 6—Based on formula used by President's Council of Economic Advisers in relation to 1964 tax cuts.

Text Of The

Amendment

Section 1. No income tax in excess of 50 per cent of net income shall be levied by Congress on the income of any corporation. Corporation dividends shall not constitute taxable income to the recipient.

Section 2. All funds raised by corporate income tax shall be distributed each year to those persons voting in the last preceding national election in equal amounts on a per capita basis. The sums so distributed shall not constitute taxable income to the recipients.

Section 3. Congress is hereby empowered to put this plan into effect on a graduated basis, but, in any event, it shall be made fully operable within five years of the effective date of this amendment.

Section 4. Congress shall have the power to suspend the operation of this plan in time of war.

Appendix

Need For Voter Eligibility Reform

In 1960, in one of the closest presidential elections in U.S. history, only 63.9 per cent of all Americans of voting age went to the polls. No less than 40 million potential voters stayed away.

In 1962, less than half the electorate voted in the off-year Congressional elections.

Undoubtedly, much of this poor record can be blamed on an amazing apathy and lack of interest in politics exhibited by many people. This is the first natural reaction to such statistics.

231

The startling fact, however, is that half of the 1960 non-voters — an estimated 20 million people — were disfranchised by outmoded registration and election laws.

Included in this number were those who were traveling or on vacation or who wore the wrong color of skin.

Five million persons were denied the right to vote because they were ill or hospitalized.

Another eight million were barred from the polls simply because they had moved some weeks or months prior to election day. They could not vote in their old or new residences.

State and local election regulations are a hodge-podge of inconsistency. Of the 50 states, 37 require one-year residence to qualify for voting; 12 require six months; one requires two years. In 46 states a voter must be at least 21 years old; in Georgia and Kentucky the legal voting age is 18; in Alaska it is 19; in Hawaii it is 20.

Also contributing to voter delinquency is the fact that most states restrict registration to one location in each county and to day-time hours. Some close registration as much as nine months before an election.

Significantly, in those few states with progressive election laws, voter turnout is far above the national average. In Idaho, for example, rather than requiring voters to report to a central office to sign up, registrars seek them out. Registration continues right up to 9 p.m. on the Saturday before a Tuesday election.

In 1960, Idaho registered 97.4 per cent of its electorate and 80.7 per cent of them actually voted.

The national dividend for every voter plan could be a giant step forward toward correcting the nation's poor voting record. In addition to eliminating apathy, which it surely would do, the plan would be certain to result in pressures for general reform and standardization of voter eligibility laws to enable every otherwise-qualified citizen to share in the dividend payments.

Index

235

237

238